God Makes Beautiful Things

LaShaneika Franklin

God Makes Beautiful Things

Copyright © 2017 by Living Word Publishers (His Kingdom Bookshelf)

All rights reserved. No part of this book may be reproduced or transmitted in any form or by any means without written permission from the author.

ISBN 13 - 978-0692859483

Printed in USA

Dedication

God has placed this book on my heart to set myself free as well as others. This book will give hope for the future. It's time to press in to the heart of Christ and see ourselves as HE sees us. I hope you enjoy and most of all I pray chains fall from you as you read and gain victory over your own personal struggles. If God did this for me, he will do it for you. This book is first dedicated to my heavenly Father. Then my earthly Father Jeff Bryant who took me in as his very own. My Uncle Steve Thornton, who is the biological brother of my biological father for always being by my side. He is the only one that keeps in contact, shows love and keeps me updated with that side of my bloodline. I want to thank my Aunt Quincy Franklin and my uncle Eric Franklin who God used as confirmation to write this book and encouraged me through the process. I thank God for their encouragement to press forward with it. Super hugs to my four daughters, Kianara, Dacia, Tiffany, Serenity, and grandson, Laquan Elijah Jr. My children have given me much motivation and courage to even tell my story to the world. I told them my life story and opened up about my battles and struggles, which also caused them to open up to me about things that happened to them; this began a healing process for us all. They even requested that I write about some of their battles and struggles, but I decided not to so that they would have a fresh chance to tell their own stories to the world. Finally, I want to thank Living Word Publishers for giving me the opportunity to share my story with the world.

Table of Contents

Introduction	8
Chapter 1: My Root of Bitterness	14
Chapter 2: Rejected and Abandoned	19
Chapter 3: Who am I?	31
Chapter 4: Granny's Baby, Church Baby	39
Chapter 5: Why does this Keep Happening to Me?	43
Chapter 6: 14 and Pregnant	49
Chapter 7: Looked for Love, but Couldn't Find It	57
Chapter 8: I Da Pappy Boss	65
Chapter 9: Minnesota Nice	71
Chapter 10: Back to Chicago	79
Chapter 11: Two Broken People won't make a Whole	88
Chapter 12: Why did we get Married?	100
Chapter 13: Lord, I Wanna be Free!	107
Chapter 14: No Devil, you won't Trick Me this Time!	121
Chapter 15: Prepare for Battle!	128
Chapter 16: Wow, I have a Purpose!	140
Chapter 17: From Larvae to Butterfly	144

Introduction

"Other people are going to find healing in your wounds. Your greatest life messages and your most effective ministry will come out of your deepest hurts." - Rick Warren[1]

We go through so many battles in this life, not realizing or understanding why. We may even go on saying, "Hey this is just a part of life, what can we do about it?" Many times, we are unaware of the spiritual things that go on in the unseen world. The unseen world is more real than the seen world. Right now, there are battles going on in the heavens for your life. These spiritual battles that we face, can be generational curses, which are spirits that are attached to your bloodline and they have gained legal ground through an open door that our ancestors have left open, through occult involvement, idol worship, rebellion, even disobedience. Then there are spiritual battles you have opened doors to in your own life, through pretty much the same portals along with many more.

I know you have heard this phrase used so much, "Give no place to the devil." Or another I have heard, "You are giving the devil way too much credit." Ephesians 4:27, this scripture is often taught wrong, and for this very reason we are mandated to study to show ourselves approved unto God, a workman that need not to be ashamed, rightly dividing the word the word of truth. What Ephesians 4:27 means is not to allow open doors for the devil to

---

[1] *Rick Warren, The Purpose Driven Life: What on Earth Am I Here for?*

enter and have free reign in our lives. Allowing anger to fester and take root, which causes sin, opens some doors. Speaking falsehood (lies) to your neighbor and if we keep on the old self that is being corrupted by its deceitful desires. While studying deliverance and demons, this was a phrase I heard a lot. But I had to explain that we are not to be ignorant of satan's devices (2 Corinthians 2:11) and inform that this teaching they heard is to keep the believers in bondage. And unfortunately, this is still being preached. See, the enemy loves darkness...so if he can stop you from talking about him or learning about him and how to defeat him, then he has already defeated you.

I know you are saying we are redeemed from the curse of the law, God has already done that for us, and the enemy is already defeated. Christ did finished works, but how do we walk in it? While Jesus was here, he gave us parables to teach us, strategies to cast the enemy out, and told us to go and make more disciples. Why would Jesus have taken the time to teach us these amazing things and we do absolutely nothing with them? After Jesus rose he told the 11 disciples in Matthew 28 to go and make disciples of all nations, baptizing them in the name of the Father, Son and the Holy Spirit and teach them everything He taught them (his disciples). What did he teach the disciples? To cast out demons, Right? Mark 16 says that, when they go out into all the world and preach the gospel, whoever believes and is baptized, they shall CAST OUT DEMONS, speak in new tongues, pick up snakes with their hands - even drink deadly poison and it will not harm them. Well this tells me I have work to do. This was not a suggestion, this is a command. Disciples are still being made and WE are still to do the same things commanded by Jesus.

The difference is, we know that the enemy is defeated but he is also a tormentor, a bully might I add. What he fears is us knowing who we are, the power and authority that we have and the spiritual legal system God has in place. If we become knowledgeable of these things and begin to operate in them, satan must cease in his maneuvers. So, casting out devils is not a nuisance and we must do this to be set free from the oppression.

I am a single mother of four beautiful young ladies; I have one son in law and one grandson. I was born and raised on the Westside of Chicago by my grandmother. I am an only child through my biological parents, but through my father who raised me I have siblings, and he still makes sure that we have a great bond. I am especially close with my little brother Jeff who I was raised in the same house with. I entitled this book God Makes Beautiful Things because after learning that no matter what wrong I did, He is using them all for my good. Even while I was doing wrong, He kept me. I am grateful and know that I owe him my life to do his will. He could have given up on me. He could have taken His hands off me, but he didn't. To whom much is given, much is required. I was a wretch undone, so far from perfect and God still loved me enough to call me out of darkness into his marvelous light!

One thing is for sure; we do not serve a powerless God. I am tired of the church being defeated by our adversary. If we are made in His likeness and His image, we are not powerless! We have power to tread upon serpents and scorpions so that we may come out of bondage and the traps the enemy has set. I know we look at our past and begin to condemn ourselves, but let me tell you, no matter what you have been through or done wrong God doesn't hold you to your past when you come into the Kingdom. God will use your story to help millions of people who have experience what you experienced. Contrary to what you believe, God needs you. He has work for you to do that will turn the kingdom of darkness upside down. Hell has feared you from the start and that's why he used the bondage you're in to keep you trapped and feeling worthless. Once you come out tell everyone about it! Your story is YOUR story, don't fear or be embarrassed to talk about it! Also, never allow anyone to discredit it - tell it. Tell it with boldness so that many more captives will be set free.

Tell God Yes!

All God needs is a yes from you, but once you say yes get ready for training. When I said yes, I also went through what is called the Wilderness season. This season is to remove distractions and move you forward in your assignment as well as trusting God even when you don't feel those goosebumps in church. Too often we become addicted to a feeling and we don't operate in faith, but faith is how God desires for us to operate. When the children of Israel were in the wilderness, they complained because Moses went away from them too long. They were used to Moses going up the mountain and coming back down whenever he went to speak with God. This last time when Moses went up, they saw the consuming fire at the top of the mountain. But then he was gone for 40 days, so they were unsure of what happened to Moses. All their faith was in Moses, but none was in God. The Israelites asked

Aaron to create them a god. He created a golden calf, even after God said more than 1 time in different ways to have no other Gods, worship no other idols, keep your eyes on me. The crazy part is, even Aaron agreed with this plan and he was a prophet! In the wilderness, it is easy to lose focus because God seems like He is not near. God is training you for reigning in the Kingdom of light. At this point He is teaching you to operate without a feeling, but with faith. Pray without a feeling, cast out demons, perform signs, wonders and miracles without a feeling, believe without a feeling and so much more.

    One thing I asked in prayer that changed my life was, "as I take delight in you, give me the desires of my heart." Many people do not understand the meaning of praying this. Some believe that this means, that He will give us all that we desired even before we chose to seek Him. All the carnal and fleshly desires that we have. Oh No. When God changes your heart, He removes your selfish desires and places His desires for your life upon your heart. Your heart will begin to break for the things that break His. He will even put a passion for your purpose there, and you will start to seek it out. Even when you pray this prayer, there is something you must do…. Open Your Heart!

    I had a dream and God spoke to me and said, "Open your heart and receive all that I have for you." I thought, "Open my heart? What does that mean?" So, I began to search out the scripture and listen to sermons regarding an open heart. God knew that if my heart wasn't open I would not have stepped out on faith, neither with this book nor the mentorship program. This is my journey from maggot to butterfly. How God turned my mess into a message, my test into a testimony. This season has been great for me and has allowed me to seek God like never before with clarity, wisdom and understanding. My relationship with my heavenly Father has given me so much joy that I desire to help so many other women find this very same joy. This is why God placed *Women of NOW Faith Mentorship* program in my spirit. So, come on and take this journey with me and see how my worst mistakes, became my greatest victories.

This book is not an autobiography but it is about the battles I have had to fight. Some are generational and some I opened the door to myself. God had me to write this book to obliterate shame, and break some chains in the family line by bringing the darkness into the light.

Battling rejection was not easy at all. This thing tried to keep its grips on me, but not so! I made lots of mistakes, lied a lot, made terrible decisions, and so much more. My desire with this book is to bring my family into revival, as well as anyone else who is reading this book. I PRAY that fear, shame, guilt and condemnation be broken off you now in Jesus name. I pray that this will cause you to bring your darkness to the light and be set free from all that has had you bound and all that have had you children and your ancestors bound. That you get courage to share your life story and struggle to help someone else in Jesus name. Amen.

Chapter One

My Root of Bitterness

Welcome to my journey. I am a 35-year-old divorced mother of 4. I have been raised in the church all my life, but I really began to pursue God with my heart about 3 years ago. I was just like most Christians today, not taking scripture and living it. My life hasn't been as good; neither has it been all the way bad. Yet when I see God moving I now understanding when people say, "What the devil meant for evil, God will turn it around for our good."

My mom and dad met in high school, where they fell in love. Honestly now, what do teenagers know about love? My dad was a handsome man. My mother was pretty and had the book smarts to go along with it. They decided after high school to move together, and things ended up shaky. My biological father became abusive toward my mother. My mom became pregnant with me, and she wanted out. So, like any woman would do…she called her parents to rescue her. After leaving my mother told my father that she was pregnant, and I am for sure she didn't hear from him anymore. She stayed with my grandparents on the Westside of Chicago along with her siblings. One that would irritate her and get under her skin, just because he could; my uncle Jay, who kept her busy at the start of her labor. There is a symptom in women when they are about to give birth. It is what my family call, "the cleaning fit," where a woman goes on a cleaning spree, cleaning everything in the house from top to bottom. So, my uncle Jay would say to his sibling, "Watch this" and go dirty up a dish and my mom, in the early stages of labor she would go grab the dish and clean it. He would do this repeatedly. Funny, right?! I could just see her now, moving fast around the house making sure everything is in its rightful spot. So, in October 5, 1981 a star was born, yours truly - me... I was something fresh for my family. I was the first niece and grandchild, so I got all the love. My uncle always told me about how I would cry (or what he would say, "holler") as a baby and he would give my mother relief when it got frustrating and he saw she need a break. It's so wonderful to have help with children, TRUST ME.

We made due as a family. Our home was quite chilly so to the point that my grandmother put the bed for my mom and I in the kitchen. They would use the oven to heat that part of the house. My mother raised me until I was 5 years old and she decided the military was the best option. My grandparents had to raise me. Now, my grandfather was still alive, but had a stroke and was not able to talk. So, he would make certain gestures and noises. It was a hard for everyone else to adjust to him not being able to speak and understand what he was saying, but not me. By the time I was born, my grandfather had been living as a stroke survivor, so his new way of communication was the only way that I had taught him. One day he was making gestures for something, my grandmother wasn't quite understanding what he was asking for. I saw him and her getting frustrated at one another. So, I yelled out, "He wants some peanuts!!" And my grandfather shook his head yes and smiled.

When my grandfather died, my mom came back from the military. That was hard for me, because she had to leave shortly after to go back and serve in the military. I remember waking up one morning and seeing my cousin who I thought was my mom. They looked so much alike. It is also a reason for that, but I will leave that story to the older generation, who knows more about it than I do.

As a child growing up I was always mild and timid. I would often get bullied. This started for me in Kindergarten. My grandmother would pick me up from school and when I tell you, she was a true Madea[2]... you better believe it. If she found out I was being picked on by anybody, she would make me stand up to whoever would call me names and do mean things to me. They would say things like, "Girl, you are Chinese" and use their hands to slant their eyes and begin to mock a Chinese language. They would also talk about my nose and say I had a pug dog nose. They said, "I bet you could smell everything." Last thing they used to pick on me about was my breathing. I'll admit after a while I did notice that my breathing was a little loud. But they would say, "Can you breathe? Dang, you got asthma or something?"

These names begin to build insecurities in me. I began to look at myself and see a big nose, Chinese looking girl. I did not like what I saw in the mirror. If my hair was off my face in a ponytail, I hated it because I had to look at my whole face. The only time I would feel good about my hair is when it was down and full of hair beads. My aunt would take her time and spend hours doing my hair. It was super thick! And did I mention I was tender headed? I became bitter at the age of 5. I would see other

---

[2] *From Tyler Perry's productions*

kids who were not being picked on and think how pretty they must be to everybody. I never seemed to fit in. I always tried. Pretty much all my life I had been trying to figure out exactly where I belong. Never finding a place of identity, also finding out the people who I called my true friends, weren't and ultimately, they never had my best interest at heart. Because of this, I began to settle for whoever would accept me as a friend. This was a pattern that went about even into my adult years.

    I kept all these feelings on the inside, bottled in shame. I just wanted to be accepted. I started to see that people would just up and walk away from me. My so-called friends would also stop playing with me for no apparent reason. I even had a friend on the block where I grew up who I loved to play with. But her mother wasn't too fond of our friendship. I mean we were just two kids, making mud pies, playing hopscotch, jump rope, but anytime her mother would see her with me she would call her back to the porch and I would ask to come in and sit with her, but her mother wouldn't allow me. I would stand on the other side of the fence and talk to her. My friend would even cry when her mother would make her go on the porch. Then I noticed my friend would have to sneak to play with me. Even at a young age I knew there was something, but I didn't quite know. I never had the courage to ask my friend why did it seem as if she was sneaking to play with me. But my grandmother filled in the blanks for me. My grandmother is and always has been blunt, will not sugar coat a word she says. She told me plainly, "That little girls mom thinks she is better than you. It is sad she won't allow you two to play together." Here comes more insecurities. Even in this situation, I began to look my outer appearance and comparing, I thought to myself, "She has long hair." I mean I have long hair, but hers is way longer than mine. She has her dad at home, I don't. Her mom is at home, my mom love me, but she lives in Germany. My friend was also a pretty girl. I began to compare facial features. "She has chinky eyes, but she doesn't have a big nose like mine. Maybe she is better than me. She has it all. A big brother too." While I was an only child, these things began to run through my head and torment me daily. I had opposition at school, in my neighborhood, and at church.

    One thing's for sure, my grandmother kept me in church. She allowed me to go to church with some friends of the family who stayed on my block sometimes. Their family had a church on Chicago Ave and Monticello. We would walk to church, just my friend, her brother and me. Before we got to church, we would always stop at the corner store and get pickled pig feet. LOL YES you read correctly, "Pig Feet." Honestly, I didn't like the way those tasted, but I would eat them with her and her brother just to fit in. I didn't feel like I belonged at the church, because no one acknowledged me there at all. I wanted to be involved and I always felt overlooked. So once again, still not finding a place where I feel accepted. Something even happened between me and that girl's friendship. I can't remember the exact details. I know I remember her brother having a small crush on me and that made her angry. Our friendship was short lived due to conflict of interest. No matter where I went I felt pushed away and this caused bitterness in me.

Chapter Two

Rejected and Abandoned

These are the spiritual strongmen that were the head commanders to destroy my life. That was until God called me by name and adopted me into Sonship. These spirits caused fear, insecurities, promiscuity, and made me my own protector as to have lordship over myself. I thought I could protect myself from being hurt over and over the same way. I would cut people off quick without a thought. Rejecting people before they even had a chance to reject me. This spirit can have you feeling a false superiority, because you dare not take any crap from anyone. You begin to look for flaws in others, more than you search yourself and your own soul. You take the heat off yourself and apply it to someone else. You take no responsibility for your actions. There is always an excuse for why you did something, all to justify your actions. Abandonment and rejection kept me from my destiny and purpose. I either gave too much too soon in a relationship, or I ran from it whenever a problem would arise. Excuse me, your rejection is showing[3]. It also caused me to stay in a relationship, thinking that would be the best I would ever have. Although I would cut people off, I would still attract people with the same spirit. We are what we attract, as the saying goes.

Honestly, I didn't know this spirit claimed my life until a few years ago. As we all do, we call what we are feeling something

---

[3] *Funny quote from Dr. Matthew L. Stevenson III*

different to soothe ourselves and to allow others to think we are okay within our situation. I truly did not know why I harbored bitterness and resentment toward so many people. Rejection and abandonment truly robs you of your identity and hinders you from coming into your predestined self, which is what the enemy fears. You only walk into your destiny when you find out your God given identity. Being rejected and abandoned over and over in life only gives that spirit stronger power over you with every rejection you experience.

    My first feelings of being abandoned came when my mother went to the army. Although she did what she felt she had to do, sometimes we don't know the effects our actions have on our children. The enemy used this as a strongman, by allowing others who would abandon me to walk in and out of my life. Even in friendship, I felt rejected and most times abandoned. As I said before, I didn't fit in with anyone or anywhere.

    When I was about 9 or 10 years old my mom asked me to move with her, now you know I was excited to go. My grandmother was hurt I was leaving and rightfully so, I had been with her all those years and now it is time for my mom to put time in. My mom came and got me and we drove in her Beretta all the way to El Paso, Texas. The ride was 2 days long. My first road trip ever. I remember stopping at a store for souvenirs. My mom asked me what did I see, that I wanted. I picked up Bobby Brown, *Don't Be Cruel* on cassette tape. Man, that was my favorite album. I listened to that daily. But anyway, we get to Texas and we have to stay with her Military buddy Larry, I called him uncle Larry. When I met him, he welcomed me with open arms; he was someone I felt safe around. He and his sons Lil Larry and Michael lived there. Lil' Larry was like a big brother to me, but Michael well that was a different story.

My first day of school in Texas I had to catch the bus, which I had never done before. My thoughts were, am I on the right bus, and will I get on the right bus to come home? I mean I was terrified. But I made it back to Uncle Larry's house safely. When I made it back, Michael was there. I tried to have a conversation with him, but he just blew me off. It was obvious he didn't want me there. He would say and do mean things to me, by pulling pranks like, locking me out the house. I would tell my uncle Larry, and Michael would get his behind tore up, or Lil' Larry would find out and go off on him for treating me that way. NONE of this stopped him though.

Lil' Larry was my heart, though. Lil' Larry was in high school and knew all the latest music. He always made sure I was alright and asked me about my day. We would sit in his room and listen to Chubb Rock and some other rappers. I remember one time he got in trouble. Not for sure what he had done, but I believe it was for bad grades. He got a good whooping from his dad and got his music taken away. It crushed my soul when this happened for 2 reasons. I didn't like him getting the whooping, I believe it hurt me more than him, plus while he was on punishment it wasn't the same. He was in his room and I was left with Michael when the adults were gone. Now rejection took a stronger grip on me.

Not only was I being rejected at the house we were staying at, but at school as well. I began making friends; well at least I thought I did. There were 3 girls that hung together and they were the first to approach me. One Hispanic girl names Leticia, but we called her Leti, another girl named Kim, the third girl I don't remember her name at all. Seemed like we hit it off well at first, but later I would have to prove myself by fighting. Kim and the other girl, whose name I don't remember, plotted a lie to have Leti pick a fight with me.

We are on the playground during recess, the girls are instigating the issue. They were telling me what Leti was saying and telling Leti what I was saying. Well honestly twisting our words so that things would escalate and they could see a fight. So we are finally face to face. I mean, Leti is all in my face talking all kinds of smack. I don't do much talking, so I hit her. As the gym teacher was running toward us the fight began. This landed us in the principal's office. While in the office, we looked at each other and we both start crying, talking about, "I didn't want to fight you." "I didn't want to fight you either." We hugged and everything - oh but that didn't stop in house detention LOL. I literally had to have a fight to be accepted. I mean, what was this, some type of initiation?

Even after that fight, I still did not feel as if I belonged. This move wasn't easy for me at all. I would fly back and forth from Chicago back to Texas. One thing about Chicago, I came back and I still had the same so called friends. I knew how far to go with them already. El Paso was just unchartered territory for me. I loved the weather in El Paso, but getting in trouble was another thing. My mom was so stern though, I wasn't used to that either. I would always tell her, "You treat me like one of your privates." She was a staff sergeant in the Military by this time. I was used to either getting my way, or being talked to in a mal-manner. Maybe even a whooping, but this was my norm. What is this "punishment" stuff? I won't lie, I felt like punishment was for white kids. She took everything; phone, television, outside privileges, you name it. I almost sank into depression sitting looking at 4 walls. My momma did not play, when it came to my grades, my attitude with others or anything. Anytime I got on punishment, I wouldn't even have to say anything, my grandmother would hear the sadness in my voice and she would tell my mom to send me back to Chicago.

I came back to El Paso at the beginning of a new school year, so me and my mom moved into a 2 bedroom, 2-bathroom apartment, second floor huge balcony. My room was "Off the chain." I had a queen-sized waterbed and my own telephone line in my room. I had the see-through phone that would light up in the inside when it rung. My mom had bought me so many stuffed animals. I also had an Atari; I was a true princess.

I started drinking at an early age; I loved Canadian Clearly at the time. My mom would buy them all the time for me, but she would purchase wine coolers for herself. Whenever there was no Canadian Clearly, I would drink her wine coolers, and she would come home and say, "who drunk my wine coolers?" (As if it was someone else there besides me and her), so my little smart butt tells her, "Well if you would buy my drinks, I wouldn't drink yours." Maybe I was drunk when I said that. Either way, that was her perfect opportunity to take me down, but she didn't, she just laughed. Honestly, this was before I knew what wine coolers were and what they contained. My granny didn't drink wine coolers, just give her a nice cold Budweiser and she was happy. So, I had no idea what a wine cooler was.

I remember seeing a Ouija board at my mom's house that was on the shelf in her closet. I immediately told her to get rid of it. I had to pressure her to get rid of it. I literally had to go into tears, after she got her laughs off, she finally threw it away. I was relieved and felt I could live another day LOL. I will discuss this later.

We had adjacent neighbors. It was a man, his wife and two daughters. The man was in the military as well. His daughters' names were Jessica and Shadé. I was close in age with Jessica, but Shadé was younger. I became friends with them. We would spend nights at one another's house. I remember her mom would literally scream her name, "JESSICA!!!!" I mean you would always think this girl was in trouble the way she would call that little girl. Anybody who knows me knows if I have to go to the bathroom at night I don't flush the toilet. The reason for this… This woman scared me straight. One night I spent the night over Jessica's house and I went to the washroom, I flushed the toilet. All I heard in a loud thundering voice, "WHO FLUSHED THE TOILET?!" I didn't say anything, but I ran back into Jessica and Shadé's room. Their mom came storming into the room, "Who flushed the toilet? Again, I stayed silent. But Jessica told her who it was. Their mom looked at me sternly and said, "we don't flush the toilet at night." I apologized to their mom and she walked out the room. I asked Jessica, what's the big deal with flushing the toilet? She told me her dad was a very light sleeper and it wakes him up. (Note to self: This is definitely something I need to be delivered from, be healed in Jesus name).

After being Jessica's BFF for a while, things became rocky between us, you know how they say, when someone shows you who they are believe them. Well these characteristics began to surface and I was a girl from Chicago and look, we don't play that. If Jessica wasn't getting her way with me, she would start to go and knock on my door and tell my mom I was being mean to her. My mom told me, I should be nice. My mom didn't get all the details, but my mom was only trying to help me keep friends by me being in a new place. After that, I saw her laugh at the fact that my mom was telling me off. But I kept trying to be her friend. I remember I had a sleepover and I invited a few of the friends I had in the complex. While having a good time, Jessica began to cry because she felt I was playing more with the other girls than her. SO again, I guess I was being mean to her. My mom told us to include her, when in fact we were trying but she didn't want to play. Boy, I think she had my mom wrapped around her finger. Another incident happened between us where she didn't get her way and sure enough she ran off to go tell my mother, and when she came back, I hit her - dead in the face. I sent her crying to her momma after that! My mom heard her crying and came out; she told my mom that I hit her. Of course, my mom asked me why, I plainly told her, "because she keep lying on me, saying I am being mean to her, all because I will not do what she wants me to do!" Our moms separated us. Jessica would be playing by herself on the steps and I would walk past her and go and play with my other friends who lived in the complex.

We stopped talking to one another and to me our friendship

was burned by fire. That's pretty much what I wanted it to be. We had a party room in the complex. This party room was literally under Jessica's apartment. Our balcony overlooked the party room's patio. Jessica was having a birthday party in there. I saw when Jessica came and dropped the invitation off to my mom. I honestly did not want to go. But my Mom brought the girl a present. In my mind, I am hoping she would just drop the present off at Jessica's house. I guess that was not my mom's plan. My mom made me humble myself and told me that I had to go to the party. When I tell you, she cried when I showed up, she balled. She was so happy that I came. I'll admit, loosened up after that, cause now my ego has kicked in. Although she may have gotten emotional and showed remorse, our friendship never went back to where it was. But at least I was now able to speak to her, sit and maybe play for a little while. I still didn't quite feel like I fit in her circle, nor did I want to. I made sure I would push her away before she had the chance to push me away or make up any other lie.

Not only did I have problems in the complex where we lived, but also in two other places, at school and at one of my mom's friend house. Let me tell you about the school and why I still didn't feel a sense of belonging. By this time, I was in middle school. This school was huge. I had only seen schools like this on movies. It was always warm in Texas, so the hallways to the classrooms were outside. Also, this was my first experience with switching classes and not having the same students in all my classes. I loved it at first. I made a few friends, so I thought. The first time I had a locker, and did not have to share a locker. For a little while I didn't use my locker I was afraid that I would lock myself out and would not be able to get back in. But after a while, those books got too heavy and I had no choice. When I go to my locker, it's not locked. There was a cool looking blue jean folder, with black straps. I leave it in there for a while. After no one had claimed the folder or removed it from of my locker, so I believed it was mine for the taking. My mom asked me where did I get it from. Look…don't judge me for my answer, I wanted to keep it. I told y'all before, she didn't play and if she knew it wasn't something she purchased herself, she was making me take it back. Okay…so I lied, I told her some people from the Dare program gave us those folders. The fabric on the folder was a little worn, so I also said it had been in their trunk for a while.

A few days later, I am in class with the folder and one of my so-called friends asked me where did I get that folder from. I was honest with her, I told her I found it in my locker. She walks away from me with this funny look on her face, but says nothing else to me. Next thing I know, I'm called to the office, and they already called my mom and asked her to show up. Her mother had also showed up to the school. They accused me of stealing it from the girl. Now mind you I had already lied to my mom about where I had got the folder from, so I truly had no defense. I was in trouble at home and had detention. My mom was so angry, but rightfully so. She got called off her job because her child had been accused of stealing. I learned a valuable lesson from this. Because had I told the truth, she probably would have had my back. I remember every time I would see the girl whose folder it was, she would avoid me at all cost. I remember this one day I didn't want to go to detention, so I went to class. The teacher looked at me and was like, "LaShaneika you are supposed to be in detention." Oh, I was so mad. I looked at the girl (she was in this class with me) and I mean mugged her so hard. I wanted to lay hands on her in such a natural way, that the stunt she pulled with me she won't ever pull again. I felt this way because after everything went down, I asked her why she didn't just say that is was hers, I would have given it to her. When I asked her this question, she mean mugged me and walked away. So, from then on, I hated the sight of her. But to make matters worse, all the kids at school were calling me thief and no one really wanted to be around me. I never made one friend there.

During the same time of the school incident, my mom had a friend who had 3 kids and after school I would go over to their house. The kids' names were, Kim, Clifford and Xavier, who we all called Zay. Kim was like a big sister to me, she would do my hair and other nice things for me. Clifford was older, but I had a little crush on him. He knew it right, so when my mom would pick me up, Clifford would give me a kiss on my cheek and say see you tomorrow. I made sure Kim did my hair cute so when Clifford saw me, he would be impressed (I was a little fast girl). But Xavier on the other hand, oh boy. He hated me being at his house. He would literally fight me, daily. I mean we would go blow for blow. His mom got on him and he would be okay if she was there, but when she wasn't, the monster came out to. He would throw things at me, call me names, hit me and we would begin fighting. This was also a rough time for me. I still did not feel accepted anywhere I went. I remember crying to my mom telling her I wanted to go back to Chicago. She didn't delay, she had me on the soonest flight back to my grandmother.

After moving back to Chicago with my Grandmother, my Aunt Ingrid enrolled me in Our Lady of Sorrows Catholic School. I was diggin' the uniforms. They were green and gray plaid skirts, white shirts, green sweater, green knee high socks and black shoes. I won't front, I thought I was cute. Secretly I had a desire to go to Catholic school, because I thought it would be like the movie "Sister Act" (don't laugh at me). Little did I know, I was in for a rude awakening. It was nothing like a sister Mary Clarence there and the teachers weren't nuns. I walked into this classroom and everybody seemed nice at first, the guys were smiling and the girls were friendly and introducing themselves. After a while I took my coat off and all the boys smiles turned upside down and the girls began to whisper. One boy, began to be rude and mean to me. One day during a back and forth argument with this young man, he looked at me and said, "all the guys in here liked you until you took your coat off!!!!"

I didn't know what he meant by that, until one of the girls at the school explained, what he meant when he said this. She knew because they were all discussing me. The young lady proceeded to tell me it, was because I didn't have any breasts. I did notice I was a bit of a late bloomer. Every girl in the class had breasts, except me. I went home and asked my grandmother to buy me some bras. So, her and my aunt went and brought them, no questions asked, even though I had nothing to put in them. So, I'm sure you know what I did next. I stuffed my bra. That didn't look right. Couldn't get them leveled out right, one would look bigger than the other. Plus, I figured they would notice, because that type of growth spurt doesn't happen overnight. But even this incident took a toll on me. Not only was I not happy with my Chinese eyes and my pug nose, now I became unhappy with my body.

This spirit of rejection followed me, no matter where I went. It attached itself so tight that I began to reject myself. I began to hate everything about myself: my hair, my face, and my body. I even felt I wasn't smart because I always had a hard time with math; I could barely get a C in that class. I became so insecure in math, because the teacher would ask a question and if I didn't know the answer I would hear snickering all over the room. I believed I was the only one struggling with math, so I felt stupid. It wasn't until college I saw some peace with math. I got more help AND I became determined to get a little out of it.

Chapter Three

Who Am I?

When my mom went to the military she gave my grandmother temporary custody of me. We stayed in a 2-flat building on Chicago's West side. I was born and raised in this house. We had neighbors on the first floor; the Moffett's, who were and are still family to us. I would play with the grandson who was about my age. This was literally the only other place I could go when I wanted to go outside. Whenever anything happened in that family, we hurt and if anything, ever happened in our family, they were hurt the same. I gained such a great connection, I called the sisters my aunties and the brothers my uncles. They looked out for me, just as my own family. They are the only ones that would call me "Neika." Everyone else called me Nikki. I love that even to this day, how they had their own way of identifying me. This was the beginning of a search, to find out where I belonged. Here is a family that has both mother and father and the kids there had their mother and fathers as well. I didn't know this would cause many personal issues in life regarding my identity.

My Aunt Ingrid is like my mom, no matter what she did she always included me. Her high school and college friends, talk about it to this day, because even when they get together right now, my aunt includes me. And we just get together and have a great time.

When I was 5 years old, my auntie Ingrid became pregnant with her own child. You would think that this would change how she treated me, but it never did. This beautiful baby boy became my little brother. His name is Jeffrey Jr. His dad would come pick us all up and we would go out and have great time. Whether picnics, football games, Easter, Christmas whatever, we were always together. I remember one day we were at a picnic and he introduced me as his daughter. After that, "he had me at hello." I began to feel like I had my own daddy. A feeling that could never be replaced, rehearsed, or faked. That statement was real for me. He had a piece of my heart, and for sure I had a piece of his.

Suddenly things changed. I remember it was right after my two aunts were in a car accident. They were on their way to their weekend job. A semi-truck hit them at an intersection. My aunt Sharon was hurt, but my Auntie got the impact and she was banged up bad. The accident caused damage to her face and eye. Now, mind you my auntie was so pretty, bow-legged and a walk that would stop traffic. She is still the same. Although it took a while for her to get back to herself, you could just imagine how hard this was for her. But I remember my dad would only come pick up Lil Jeff and not me. I would ask him could I go, and he would say, "MAYBE, next time..." This would absolutely hurt my soul. I began to think maybe he didn't want me anymore either. This didn't stop me from asking could I go though. I continue to press him until he eventually asked my aunt Ingrid if it would be OK, and she said yes. My persistence and desperation broke him down. He may have even seen the sadness and got tired of watching the tears and it hit him somewhere in his heart.

My dad still didn't pick me up, every time he picked up Jeffrey. But this was something that began to bother me. I saw that everyone else I know had their parents or at least a mother at home and here I am with Aunties, Uncles, and by this time only a grandmother. My Grandfather had passed already when I was around 6 years old. Even my Uncle Jay and Auntie Quincy had kids. Their kids also have their parents, so what makes me so different? So, during the time I wasn't getting my dad's Big Jeff's attention as much as before, I began to look at my aunt Quincy and uncle Jay for parenting. My auntie Ingrid was right there never left, but it is something about that masculine/fatherly love toward a little girl. I thought I would look to them for that, which was short-lived because I noticed, once again, I was out of place. They would do things with their kids and I would not allow me to tag along. Not that they didn't love me, but me being a child and searching, I didn't understand.

After I was prompted to stop asking people to go along with them, my fight became internal. Thoughts began in my head, about how I don't fit in, they don't want you around.

My dad Big Jeff would still come and pick me up, every so often and we would have a great time together. If you don't think kids pay attention to detail, you better think again. The one and only time my heart was broken was when he got married. It wasn't the fact he was getting married, it was that he did not include me in the wedding at all. I was in the pews at the wedding. I secretly cried about it, never voiced my opinion of it, too prideful to even ask, can I be in the wedding or even be in the wedding pictures. Even as a child, in my mind, I'm like don't they see me? Why am I invisible right now? That was another war that went on inside my head; the fight to keep my dad, MY Dad. I thought I was losing him to this marriage, so when Jeffrey said daddy was coming to get him too. Oh, he didn't know, but he was coming to get me too.

I would have my clothes packed and ready to go when Big Jeff, showed up. OK… this sometimes worked, not all the time. But I still wasn't about to lose the person I could call Dad to a marriage or anything else. Then, on weekends that he couldn't take me. He would call me to the trunk of the car and open the trunk, and fill my pockets with money. That got me through a few hours, because once the money was gone, I still wanted to be out south with them. He was all I knew as a father.

At this point I am still a young child, in my teens and I began to look for love in all the wrong places. Dating began early, which I will also discuss later in Chapter 6. But this is where my search became relevant and I wanted to know where I fit in, or do I make my own place to fit it. When you feel, you can find your identity in a human being, you lose sight of everything. Walking around blindly on a search. We believe we can find our identity in our earthly parents, not realizing that they are flawed, and if we looked to them for that, it can only make things worse. Let me explain. Some people have their parents in their life and are not feeling loved and cared for. They may see their mom being abused by their Father, or parents are alcoholics, one if not both, or drugs and this too can cause identity problems. No one can reach their potential with this type of dysfunction and growing up in this type of environment can have effects on people in the latter years. These are the same attacks satan uses to keep you stagnant, and beneath who you were created to be. Trying to find identity in people who don't know who they are, and whose they are only makes us just as messed up, if not worse.

See the right father figure in our lives do matter. Prophet Kevin Leal said, "Dysfunctional Dads, make Demonized Daughters…" When we don't have the right father figure in our lives, this will make it a struggle to receive THE FATHER'S LOVE. I am talking about the love of Christ. We look at him as our earthly fathers, here one day and absent the next. So, when God says, "I will never leave you nor forsake you" we don't understand this and the enemy builds on that. Because I messed up today Jesus is going to walk away from me, just like my daddy did. And this is not, so although this doesn't happen overnight in anyone who is fatherless or has had dysfunctional fathering, it can be done. You can be made whole and delivered from this spirit of abandonment and rejection.

My Dad, Big Jeff, is an amazing man. He took on a responsibility that he did not have to. I am so grateful that God put him in my life to be a father figure, because right now, he is so much more than a father. This began after I got pregnant with my oldest child. And he has not changed. Our Father and daughter relationship seems to grow more and more even now. I can talk to him about literally any and everything, he is a jokester but he has sound advice and he has never judged me. Nothing but pure love comes from him and my little Serenity is Paw Paw's baby (the grand kids call him Paw Paw). Whenever I say we are going over my Dad's house, Serenity gets excited and starts singing "We going to my paw paw house."

If I were a Bird

Back to the search, one more incident as an adult that cause me pain. I was 23 years old and my aunt Ingrid and I decided we would find my biological father. This plan was thought of over some Vodka and Miller High life. Once the drunkenness came down, I thought on this thing and eventually began my pursuit. I was working at a law firm as a secretary, Robins, Kaplan, Miller & Ciresi in Minnesota. I looked him up on the Internet, but couldn't find him. I remember my aunt saying that he had brothers that also went to the High School that my parents attended. I was on classmates and Black Planet websites at the time and found another Kemp that was handsome, light skinned and attended their high school around that time. I emailed him and told him that I believe he may know my father Chris Kemp. He dated my mom in high school and I was searching for him. I gave the number to the law firm just in case I had reached some psycho I didn't want him with my true information

After a few days, I got no response so I gave up on that search. But after about a week I got a telephone call at work. I answered the telephone and on the other line, the person asked for me, I said, "this is her, how may I help you?" He said "it is Chris Kemp. You reached out to my brother." I began to sweat and shake. I asked him to hold for one minute I would need to pick the call up in a private room somewhere. As I put the call on hold, I began to wonder if this was even real. The man on the other line sounds like he is white. He doesn't sound black, maybe this is some type of joke. Somebody else done got a hold of my email and wanted to play a cruel joke. But I decided I would talk to the guy and get more information. I told my co-worker to cover for me while I go take this call in the break room. I pick up the telephone and the conversation begins. He tells me more about himself, like how he just left Minnesota himself and moved to Skokie, Illinois with his brother. Then, he says something, so profound I knew he was my baby biological Dad. He apologized for what did to my Mother.

We started talking daily and got to know one another. Our first formal meeting was at his brother's house in Skokie. It was Thanksgiving, so I met that side of my family. My uncles (especially my favorite one that has never left my side, my uncle

Steve), my cousins, and even my grandmother. My grandmother gave me a fur coat that I never wore I gave it away 10 years later. Two years ago. I became acquainted with my family, learned a little family background. Found out that my grandmother had given her boys up for adoption, which this caused a lot of problems for them growing up and being abandoned. Hmm is this thing generational?

By this time, I was preparing to move back to Chicago and Chris said he was willing to come to Minnesota to help me back and get myself situated. A couple of weeks before I were to relocate back to Chicago, I came to Chicago for a weekend. My biological father and I made a plan to catch the greyhound bus back to Minnesota together. I spoke to him the first day I got in, let him know I would be on the Westside with my Cousin trying to get things for my move back. Chris did ask me to come see him, but once my cousin Dondrell was done taking me to make all the rounds I needed to make, he did not feel like taking me to Skokie. I told my Dad Chris that I wouldn't be able to get over there to see him, I would just see him when we leave the next day.

The next day came and I was calling my Dad Chris to make sure he was ready and what time did he want to meet at the station. I never got an answer. I called his brother, my Uncle Steve, to find out if he had talk to Chris. My Uncle Steve informed me that he had not. (I found out later that my uncle Steve had spoken with my Dad Chris and he (My dad Chris) decided not to come back with me. My uncle kept this from me because he knew how it would hurt.) I kept calling and got no answer.

By now, it was time to get to the Greyhound bus station. Even when I got there, I was looking for him. He knew the exact time the bus was supposed to pull off. I looked for him until the bus pulled off. Needless to say, he never showed up. I was devastated, heartbroken. I put my headphones on and pulled my cover over my head. "If I Was a Bird" by Floetry played on repeat and the tears just flowed from my eyes all the way back to home. This is how I felt, I just wanted to fly completely away. Rejected again and didn't know why. I found out later that he didn't show up, because I wasn't able to go and see him that weekend, so he was actually mad at me, for something I had no control over. I didn't have my own car, PLUS I was on business, not pleasure during this visit.

Chapter Four

Granny's Baby, Church Baby

Yes, I was a granny baby, Leona's baby. Raised by a southern woman, who knew things. I know she had a prophetic gifting. She would tell me about everybody that I knew. She would know who were my real friends and those who would betray me later. All she had to do was look at them. So, in my thoughts I felt like she was judging, but even if it took years to manifest, what she said came to past. I would see my longtime friends do exactly what she said they would do. Betray me in some type of way.

My Grandmother wasn't attending church at first, but she made sure I went and when my little brother Jeff got old enough, she would send us both. The first church that we became members of was Christian Love Missionary Baptist Church, where Elder Dr. Steve Nelson was the Pastor until he passed away in 2016. When my grandmother joined the church, something changed in her life. She didn't drink anymore, I would see her read her bible daily, and she never missed a service. She seemed to be one of Pastor Nelson's biggest supporters. I will admit, I used to feel like, "Oh my God, here she goes again. It doesn't take all that." But once I got older, I listened to her testimony and saw God for myself. My tune changed and I realized it does takes all that and more. Learning that we all have a story and if we chose not to be quiet can help someone else.

I really don't remember anything from my very early years, ages 1 to 5 is pretty much a blur. Almost seem non-existent, but I know I did. It is almost as if something happened that wasn't right. I am asking God to reveal those things and He will soon. I remember doing something at such a young tender age, it had to be introduced to me in some way. It was the start to my promiscuity in my life. What I would do as a toddler, was rub my genitalia on a pillow. I remember someone asking what was I doing. I remember my grandmother saying, "leave her alone, she is just in her world…" I was Granny's baby. if I was content, so was she.

As a child, I had a horrible burning sensation in my genital area. My grandmother would literally take me in the bathroom lay me across her lap wash me down and apply Vaseline. I would ask her why that happens and what she would tell me, is that I had a hernia. After doing research on Hernias and my own daughter Tiffany being born with an umbilical hernia I can't seem to find and validity as to why and if an umbilical hernia could cause genital pain or burning. Nor do I remember frequent visit to a doctor to have this checked on. The pain after a while went away and never came back. Never had any bulge in my abdomen or in my groin area. I know I was told I was born with an umbilical hernia and that my mom taped my navel down with a silver dollar until it was completed healed. So, I find this to be odd and I would like some understanding and clarity.

Thanksgiving 2016, having a conversation over dinner with my uncle Eric I brought this very issue up, of what my grandmother called "Getting into my world." I knew he would remember the act, but what he doesn't remember is, whenever he would see me do this, he would have a look of disgust in his eyes. He wouldn't say anything to me because my grandmother would tell him to leave me alone. So, it was just looks from him, for a little while. What he doesn't know is he is the one who helped me realize it was something wrong with what I was doing. I began to get embarrassed and rather than doing it in the open, I would do it behind closed doors. I would go find a solitude spot. My Uncle doesn't remember, but he snuck up on me one day and caught me. Perfect timing, nobody was home but him and me. He now had his opportunity to get what he felt about that perversion off his chest. Boy, he called me nasty and everything!! But this helped. He helped me understand that something is not right about that. And that it should not be overlooked.

I am a Granny's baby because she spoiled me that way. Not to say it was always right, because it had many flaws. A couple things that were good that came out of being a Granny's baby was that I never had to hide anything from her. I felt I could talk to her about anything, and I did. When it came to clothes, shoes etc., it was whatever I wanted. Truly spoiled. She never let anyone say anything bad about me, not even my mother. Let me tell you, it would be so funny, when she would call my mom to complain to her if I did something wrong, but if my mom said one thing she didn't like to me, my grandmother would cut my mom right off and be like that's enough. Especially if my mom was yelling at me, hurting my feelings and I would start to cry, my Grandmother would again take the phone and have sympathy. I think she was more hurt than I was. I probably should have gotten slapped, beat, and hung by my toenails. But Grandma was always my refuge; my shelter in any type of storm. No matter what was wrong, even if I would come to her and talk negative about myself, she always lifted me up, with an encouraging word.

Chapter Five

Why Does This Keep Happening to Me?

The enemy had it in for me, because he feared what I would become. For the devil to go through all this trouble, I was truly marked by God since before he placed me in my mother's womb. Not only did he try to bring the spirit of rejection, but also put many other spirits on assignment against my life. When I was young I remember having a recurring dream almost every night. To me it was a nightmare. This little green man would tie me down to a chair and torment me with laughter. I was in this empty room, scared and afraid. My hands and feet were bound and my mouth was taped shut. In 2016, the Holy Spirit gave me this verse regarding this dream, Matthew 12:29 Or again, how can anyone enter a strong man's house and carry off his possessions unless he first ties up the strongman. Then he can plunder his house.

As I told you in the previous chapter about the masturbation with a pillow at such a young age, so this perversion spirit didn't stop there. It became more aggressive by causing others to violate me. The first incident was with a peer. My aunt put me in ballet class with her friends' daughter. We would all see each other frequently. But things got strange after a while. We would be at her house and she would close her room door, and say, "let's play a game," so she calls me in the closet, and we were playing, a little rough housing and she ended up putting her hands between my legs. After a few minutes, I was comfortable and I went out the room to where my aunt and her mom was. I was ready to go. That evening ended in an argument between her and me, then a second time over her house. I didn't go in the closet, oh no! We had to go to sleep. The adults were having their time. We were now lying down in the room. I fell asleep, but woke up to her hand between my legs. I again told her to stop. She apologized, because she didn't want me to go tell. I didn't tell on her. But God was so good, we weren't going over her house that much after this. Then she moved to her grandmother's house. I would go over there sometimes, but her grandmother watched us like a hawk so, I felt safe knowing that we won't have to argue about touching me. This was the first incident to being molested as a child. The enemy went a step further and tried to cultivate an attraction for women, God blocked it.

Then it would happen again, this time with a grown man. After my grandfather passed away, my grandmother stayed single for a couple years. She decided to get some work done on the house. She hired some construction workers to do the outside of the house. We had an enclosed back porch, which had about 5 windows. I remember looking one of the windows and all I saw was this man, with a mini Afro, he smiled at me. Scared me so, I jumped straight out of the window. I began to see more of this man, almost daily. By this time, my grandmother had the basement fixed up. I noticed my Grandmother had taken a liking to this man. His name was Walter. He seemed nice at first, took care of the house and always cooked. He would pick my little brother Jeffrey and I up from school and take us to McDonalds and Burger King. My little brother wanted McDonalds and I wanted Burger King. Told you, I was granny baby, she always made sure I had it "my way." LOL

Everything seemed fine, until one day Walter and I were home alone, and he told me to come and sit with him. It went from me sitting next to him, to me sitting on his lap and then laying down with him on the couch. The first few weren't when the molestation started. Truthfully even, when my grandmother seen that, she should have stopped it, but she didn't. After a while of this, he had gained trust as well as my grandmother's' trust I believe, he then started to put his hand between my legs and began to molest me. This happened for a long time, because I was afraid to say anything.

After a while I was tired of it and I began to get more and more uncomfortable. My Aunt Ingrid would always question me about being touched. I told my auntie after a while, that Walter was touching me. Later, that night I was awakened out of my sleep, by a few people. My Auntie Ingrid, I believe it was my Uncle Bernard and for sure my Daddy Big Jeff. My Dad big Jeff was so angry. He pretty much threw my Rainbow Brite doll at me, yelling "Show me what he did..." I began to cry. This is all that I remember about that night. After that, Walter was never able to be around me again. My grandmother didn't leave him, but she kept him away from me. He was no longer even allowed in the same apartment with me. He stayed in the basement.

During this same time frame, I was going to Walter's family house for the weekends and whenever I didn't have school. I was close with his Niece Tasha. She was a little older than me, but I would spend the night with her. She would go out sometimes late at night and I would be sleep and Walter's Nephew had also begun to touch me. I would wake up to Walter's nephew with his hands between my legs. Again, I feared saying anything. After a while I just didn't want to go back over there too much if Tasha was too busy. I was attacked double at this point. But there was a spirit of perversion attached to that family.

    Then in 8th grade I moved with my Mother to the North side of Chicago. She is no longer enlisted in the Military and ready to live a normal civilian life. My mother started dating this man named Jeff. Coincidentally his name was Jeff, although he was not like my daddy Jeff. I was never too fond of him, at all. He and my mom seemed to be OK, though. Until one day he got drunk and my little sister Nicole and I were lying in the bed asleep. Well, I was asleep, but she was awake. He came into my room and I woke up to his hand between my legs. He looked at me and said, "Shh." I jumped up and said, "H*** no!" My mom heard me, yell her name. She ran out of the room and I told her what he did. She asked him why, but he grabbed her around the neck and said, "You gonna believe her over me!" My little sister and I started yelling and screaming about to help fight him with my mom. But he let her go and, she looked at us and calmed us down. She asked us if we wanted to go back over my sister Nicole's house. We both said, "Yes." We contacted her mom and she came and got us.

    The next morning my Mom came and got me and said it was time to come home. I asked my Mom if Jeff was gone. She said we would talk. When we got back to our apartment, Jeff was still there. She asked me to sit down to apologize. I sat down and Jeff was crying, he said, "I am sorry, but I thought that you were your Mom…" (I thought to myself, why would she be in my room, in my bed). Then my mom looked at me and said, "What goes on in this house stays in this house." Meaning I better not tell anyone. This is when resentment set in.

I began to resent my mother, because when it was my Grandmother's boyfriend Walter molesting me, she was ready to kill him. She came to visit from the Military after the incident and slept on the couch by the door with her gun under her pillow in case Walter walked in, but when it was her man, I had to keep quiet. I didn't feel it was fair, nor a loving move of a parent. She only allowed me to lock my bedroom door.

Eventually I told my Grandmother, I told her don't tell my mom I told her. She said she won't and she stuck to her promise. Right after I told my grandmother what happened, she asked my Mother to allow me to come back to her house. Again, my mom did not hesitate to let me go. The main reason I told my grandmother was because Jeff had begun to get drunk and fight my mother regularly. She said she wouldn't leave him. Until after I left, I ended up going to see my Mother for the weekend and my Mom and Jeff had a fight. She was in the hallway. My mother's eye was blood shot red, but she had already called the police, and she was in the hallway talking to them when I walked up. She asked me, if she should press charges, I said, "YES!" And this was the end of my mother's abusive relationship.

These are the episodes of my body being violated, it opened me up to promiscuity of my own. All my childhood, this spirit was after me and plundering my destiny, taking a deeper hold of me with ever violation. You wonder how could this happen to someone so much. It's called "Mass Molestation," a tactic of the enemy to keep one bound with fornication, fear, unforgiveness, insecurities, resentment and much more. I began to even wonder if this was something normal, because I had friends who had been molested or worse raped. Getting older I began to become saddened and depressed by these episodes. I had daughters of my own and God forbid if they need help with any of this I need to get over all of this, because I am going to have to be there for them. What if my kids go through something I need to be able to help my kids get through it. I found a therapist when I was living in Minnesota. I would attend sessions weekly and lay on her couch, just to rehearse what I had been through. It helped me to forgive my Mother but the residue and scars from these events were still there. Having resentment for my mom only caused me to feel more disconnected, more than I had already felt before the incident. I was also more fearful of her than anything, which caused me to be dishonest on numerous occasions. I remember changing my grades in 8th grade. As I said before, it was hard for me to get good grades in Math. I got a "D" in math and was scared to bring that report card home. When I tell you, I turned that "D" into a "B" real quick! Didn't know that when you are a child of God, you don't get away with much if at all anything. I got caught in everything. And would be mad cause I got caught, the foolery. Not thinking, we had parent teacher conference this marking period. My mom came up to the school. And the teacher showed her the real report card. I couldn't do anything but hold my head down. My Mom tore my butt up and put me on punishment. I deserved it all and then some.

Chapter Six
14 and Pregnant

At 14, I realized I had a lot of freedom, more freedom that I ever allow my own kids at that age. I know we say, times have changed, but that is no excuse for the lack of boundaries in any teenager's life. It was summer, right after graduating 8th grade, me and my neighbor decided to go to the show. Now this Movie Theater was about 45 minutes away from our house on public transportation. We get to the Theater and we are in our seats waiting on the movie to start. We see two young teenage guys watching us. So, my friend and I are looking back at them. They're smiling, so we're smiling back. One asked could they come and sit with us. It was room next to us, so we allowed privilege. Instead of watching the movie, we just talked until the movie was over. They asked us for our numbers. I gave the one who was interested in me, the house number, his name was Joseph. He called me as soon as I got home. We stayed on the phone almost all night. Well until my Aunt Ingrid woke up and told me, it was time to get off the phone.

  We got very close. He went to school near his house and I went to school all the way across town. But that didn't matter to him. He would get on the North Ave bus every day to come pick me up from school. Joseph always met me at the train station and would get me all the way home and then he would go home. I mean it could be freezing outside and that didn't matter to him, he would drop me off at my front door and then he would go back to his house that he had to take two buses from my house to get back home. The bad part about this is, he would skip his last classes make it to my school. I found that out later, once his mom and grandmother found out and he got in trouble.

He introduced me to his family, and then I introduced him to mines. I couldn't introduce him to my mom because I knew she wouldn't approve. My mom found out my grandmother was allowing Joseph to come and visit me at my house. When I would visit my mother's house on the North side, Joseph even came to visit me there, but my mom never knew and if she did, I probably wouldn't have been alive to tell this story. If she came to my Grandmother's house and saw him there, she would instantly make him leave and go home. Now that I have my own girls, I understand why and she was right to do that. I was only 14 with unsupervised visits from a hormonal teenage boy. My Grandmother's argument to this was, "If I allow him to come over here at least I know where she is."

After so long of us dating, I really felt like he loved me, and he felt like I loved him. Then we became intimate with one another sexually, and very soon after I became pregnant. Looking for love in all the wrong places can and will cause you to make horrible decisions. Being a teen I thought I knew it all and nobody else knew anything about love. Nobody ever taught me the spiritual consequences of having sex. I didn't even know there was such a thing, nor did my family, they were ignorant to this device of satan's bondage. They thought they were making the right decision with me. They did the best they could with the knowledge they were given. Yet, now me nor my family will no longer live in this ignorance, but we are fighting back. My mom just said, "NO! You're too young," even though she told me to come to her when I felt the urge to have sex and she would put me on birth control. My grandmother didn't speak about sex to me, not much at all, but what she did say was, "You are not a wooden pole, and you are going to have these feeling, they are natural." My grandmother made this statement after I became pregnant.

I was lying on my little brother Jeffrey's bed and my grandmother looked me in my face and said, "YOU'RE PREGNANT!!" I didn't respond. All I could think about was how did she know that I was even sexually active. By this time, it was more than once, let me remind you, I'm only 14. My goodness, this woman knows too much. By this time my Mother had moved on the 1st floor of my grandmothers building. So, my Grandmother, said, "I am going to let your mother know, she needs to take you to the clinic." This scared me, I burst into tears telling my grandmother, crying out, "NO, NO, NO!!" My grandmother told me to calm down, she was going to go sit and talk to her, and then she would send for me. I don't know what she said to my Mom, but whatever she said it worked, and my Mom was more relaxed than I had ever seen her before.

The next morning my Mom took me to Fantus Clinic. They asked me to urinate in a cup, then they sat my mom and me in an exam room where waited on the physician. He walked in, sat down looked at my mom and said, she is pregnant. Honestly, stupidly I didn't know what to feel, I thought I was in love. Then the doctor did pelvic exam and said I was only about 2 weeks pregnant. It was very early and told my Mom we had time to decide if we want to keep or terminate the pregnancy. We said NO!

Later on that day, I was on the phone with Joseph, by this

time, my mom had contacted his mom and let them know the verdict, and they weren't surprised of course. But my Mom came upstairs and saw I was on the phone and she asked, "Who are you on the phone with?" The stupidity in me responded. "The father of my child," with a smile on my face. Boy, any other day she would have slapped that smile right off my face, but she just bit her tongue and walked away.

My grandmother began to allow him to spend the night. By this time my mother had moved out. She was not standing for him spending the night. His Grandmother would have to tell him sometimes to come home. It was times too, when he just wanted to stay, he would leave out and then come back, with an excuse saying they were shooting on the next block. Knowing we haven't heard any shots LOL. But it got to a point where I began to need just a little air. I mean, we seen each other day and night, so I decided to go and spend a weekend at my Dad's house. This is when things really began to change.

Joseph grew up without his father in his life, but we knew where he stayed. His father stayed about 5 blocks away from my house. I told him, he should try to gain a relationship with his father side of the father. When he did, I wouldn't hear nor see him for weeks at a time. His grandmother would call looking for him and he wasn't at my house. Now I don't regret that I told him to grow a relationship. But it was hurtful how it seemed he forgot all about me. The trust was almost obsolete, the humor was gone and most of our time was spent in silence if we were not arguing. He made me cry with his actions, I made him cry with my words.

I did the rest of the pregnancy on my own. When I was 42

weeks, overdue my Midwife at UIC Medical Center decided to induce my labor. My mom was my support during delivery as she was at every birth, except for the last child I had. She was an amazing birthing coach. I had my oldest daughter Kianara "Keke" Franklin on September 4th, 1996. I stayed with my mom for a while after the baby was born because she had more room at her house for us.

When I had my daughter, the doctors diagnosed her with a Polycystic Kidney. They hadn't allowed my baby in the room with me my whole visit in the hospital. Then they told me she wouldn't be able to come home with me. Anyone that has carried a child and has to face the fact that the baby is not able to come home with them will begin to feel sad and empty. This was devastating news for me. As I got ready to go home on the day I was being discharged, I was in the bathroom showering. I cried most of the day because I didn't want to leave my baby in this hospital. I hear my room door open, and someone walking in sounding as if they are pushing a cart or something. Then I hear, "Mommy, I brought your baby." She was foreign. I jumped out the shower as quickly as I could and flung open the door and looked at the child to make sure that was my baby, because I was confused as well as happy, because they had told me she wouldn't be able to come home with me. Sure enough it was my Keke. I looked at the nurse and asked, "I can take her home?" And the nurse responded yes, with a smile and a head nod. That day my life was changed forever

The most hurtful thing after the baby was born was that her Father waited weeks to come and see her. He kept saying he was coming, but wasn't showing up. His Grandmother came when we got home, the hospital said to call her if we needed anything. I had a 6-week maternity break and would return to school and I chose Joseph's Great-Aunt to be her caretaker. She gave Keke the nickname "Ms. Keke." After seeing Joseph every day, we decided to try the relationship one last time.

After a while of living with my Mother, things went bad. I had a curfew, which I had to adhere to. But that wasn't the problem, I made curfew and she always knew where I was. As a matter of fact, I barely went anywhere after I had my daughter. I would only go to Joseph's house, my grandmother's house or my uncle's house, which was close to my mother's house. One day I was over Joseph's house and usually he would catch the bus home with the baby and me and then go back home. But this time, his grandmother said that she would take us home, so we called my mother and let her know that Joseph's grandmother would bring me and Keke home. She said, "okay, no problem," so I get home around 15 minutes after curfew. His grandmother took her time taking me home because she had talked to my mother and informed her that we would be a few minutes late and since she was home from work that evening and didn't feel comfortable with us getting on the bus. Joseph walked me to the door that evening and my mom seemed happy. She smiled at me, smiled at them said a few words to Joseph and he left. After they were gone I went into the room to undress the baby. My Mother comes into my room, looks at me and says, "Didn't I tell you to be home at a certain time?!" I said, "Elaine called you and told you she was bringing me home." She said, "But what did I tell you?!" And began hitting me. She was hitting me in my face, while trying to block her from hitting me in my face repeatedly. I eventually swung back. She looked at me and said, "Oh you gone hit me back?" Now I said "NO" out of fear. It wasn't my intention to ever hit my mom back. So, she said, "You wanna go live with your grandmother." You know what I said, "YEP!" I felt like she had snapped, cause one minute she smiles the next thing I know she in my room swinging on me, while I have my baby in my arms. I could never wrap my head around what was going on. My whole thought process was getting out of there while I could. She had me pack some of our stuff and she dropped me off at my grandmother's house.

That altercation with my mother made me feel like, see had a lot of anger toward me, maybe because of the embarrassment she felt through me being pregnant at such an early age or maybe it was just personal. Now I know I wasn't the best teenager, I did things like gave Joseph my baby picture and she found out, I changed my grades on my report card once, I mean I know I did things to anger my mom. With that being said, if you mad, then express that from the start. It was very confusing, because she had the chance to tell me to get on the bus, I want you home by the time I told you and not a minute later. I mean, here me on this, we explained to my mom that we would be a few minutes late, and she said, "Okay." Even when I told Joseph and his grandmother what happened, they couldn't understand it because his grandmother had spoken to my mom and she seemed all right with the plan.

Having a baby at 14 years old does not make you an adult. You are just a baby yourself. I mean, I couldn't buy a diaper if I wanted to. I wasn't even old enough to get a job. Although Joseph was old enough to get a job, he didn't from the start. We relied on our families to take care of us, plus this baby we have brought into this world. Sleepless nights if she was sick, days I didn't feel like getting up for school. I couldn't come and go as I so desired. When I get ready, now I have 2 people to get ready. Sorry but having a baby at 14 doesn't make you grown, but it does snatch your youth. Momma's baby, Daddy's maybe. Momma is always there, but daddy, well…. Maybe.

Joseph and I's relationship ended shortly after I moved back to my grandmother's house. The disappearing acts started up again. I hadn't seen Joseph for a week, but suddenly on this warm summer night he shows up at my house. At this point I was through, it was over, stick a fork in me, I was done. He walked past me and went straight into the house. Usually after he shows up from a disappearance if I am outside, I follow him inside. This time I didn't. I even had company on the porch. I stayed outside with my friends both male and female. Once I came inside, he asked me, so you stayed outside with your little boyfriend. I thought to myself, "Whatever, this Negro wants to pin blame on me because of whatever he does." I didn't even respond to that statement. The next day, he left again. This time I told him to not come back. We argued so, it almost resulted in a fight. But we just ended the relationship and he left the house.

Chapter Seven

Looked for Love, But Couldn't Find It

After I broke up with my child's father, I decided that I wouldn't stop there. As a matter of fact, I was pretty much encouraged to go out and enjoy my life. What I was told was, "Life don't stop here," or, "One monkey don't stop no show!" In those exact words. I began to date again and at this point I'm 15 years old and still have no idea who I am. There was this neighborhood rap group, they called themselves "3DB" and they were well-known, good kids, and didn't cause any trouble at all in the neighborhood. You could say I grew up with them, they just weren't my everyday group of friends. One of them that were quiet never said anything to me, but "Hi." It was summer and I was walking to the store and one of the rappers that I knew stopped me and began to whisper, "Hey Nikki, my boy like you, he thinks you're pretty." I asked him, "Who?" He told me it was Fred. I thought about it, now Fred was kind of cute. I told him, the next time I see Fred I will flirt with him. Just to let him know that I too was interested, because I am never the first to approach a man.

A few days later I am walking down Huron Street and I see Fred riding a bike, while he was riding by me kind of slow, I caressed his face and said, "Hey cutie." He smiled and kept riding. The next day, we were at the neighborhood park, and he approached me and we exchanged numbers. We met up almost daily at the park. He would help me with my baby all the time. My daughter and I became a part of his family. Fred's sister and I became best friends as well. As the relationship began to progress, I would spend nights at his house but I would tell my grandmother I was spending the night with his sister, which was where I would start my night, but it didn't end there.

    We had our own clique and although we didn't cause any trouble, we were far from perfect. It was the group 3BD, which consisted of four males, two of their other neighborhood male friends and then us four ladies, me Annette, Denise and Victoria. I began to hang with the girls tough, mostly every day. There were times we would ditch school and we would either go to my house and hang out there with my Auntie or we would walk to Humboldt Park. I mean even in the freezing cold. This is where I had my first real alcoholic beverage, because we would take Paul Masson with us to keep us warm. For those who do not know, Paul Masson is a whiskey. I began to do things, once again just to fit in. I am the one who goes to church, sing in the choir, never miss a bible class and attend every church outing. One day the guys and girls were together and we are just hanging out. I ventured into smoking a black and mild cigar (Hell has mentors too). My friend looked at me and said, "Hey Nikki, you want to hit the black." At first, I said no, but he was like, "Come on, you won't get addicted to this." So, after him saying, "Come on." so many times, I went and smoked the black and mild cigar. He taught me how to inhale, hold it, and then exhale. I didn't like it at first, but it grew on me. I would take a pull of someone's black and mild whenever we'd get together and have our drinking sessions. Eventually I started purchasing my own cigars. Then that quickly graduated into cigarettes. Our Clique began to grow. We added three more friends; two of them were Renetta and my best friend Keisha.

So now I am drinking AND smoking cigarettes and hiding my habit from my family. The cigarettes became a real live habit. I remember when I would be at home, I would go in the bathroom to smoke. The window was right over the tub. I would stand in the tub with the window open, hold my head outside the window and smoke my cigarette. Almost got caught a few times by my grandmother.

Fred and me we were together for a long time. He even escorted me to my senior prom. After prom things took a turn for the worst. Fred began to seem distant and less interested in me. We broke up a couple times but would get right back together. By this time, we were carrying devices called a pager. I would page him and he would call back, but that slowed down and often would not get a return call back. Then I began to see a strange number that would come across his pager. Whatever number I didn't recognize, I would call back, before he could. When I tell you my mind at that time was so dope, I could look at the number once and memorize all 7 digits. Why I couldn't do that in school? I was horrible at math (don't judge me). I still don't understand how that was even possible. I would call this number back and of course it was other women. I would confront Fred and we would argue, and then he would apologize and we would be back to normal for a little while at least.

It didn't stop there though. My friend was dating one of the guys as well, as a matter of fact, a few of us had coupled up by this time. But things began to be more apparent that Fred was okay being the player that he was. They would invite these girls over to the spot where we all would hang out. It was one of our friend's basement apartments. We called it "THE PAD." The guys would lie and tell us that they were going to the studio and that we had to go, because they were going to lock up. We did find that very strange because they didn't have any problem leaving us girls down there before, but now suddenly, things have changed.

I remember one day they put us out, we were coming from the store and we decided to take a shortcut walk through the gangway of our friend's house to get to the next block. We saw the lights on and heard music, so we figured they were back. We knocked on the window and everybody got quiet. My friend and I looked at one another furious. But we walked away and we decided to go back an hour later and just listen at the window. Instead of just hearing music, we heard voices and it wasn't just hearing their voices, we heard women voices as well. Come to find out they were putting us out to have other females come over. You could imagine the problems this caused. But we didn't walk away from these guys because the lack of love we had for ourselves influenced us to stay in relationship with them.

My friend and me, we often called each other Pinky and the Brain, because whenever it came down to these guys we were dating, there was nothing they could get past us. We always find a way to catch them up. I always tell this story because it is hilarious, so I am going to tell it to you. Me and my friend Annette got together and thought up a plan to catch them in the basement with these women. When the opportunity arose, we jumped at it. Once again, they said they were going to the studio and we had to leave. My friend looked at me and said, "Are you thinking what

I'm thinking, Pinky?" I said. "I think so, Brain..." We had this amazing plan. We would leave out, then we would go back and act as if I had lost my pack of cigarettes in the basement. They would let us in to look, while I am in the basement looking, my friend would run upstairs to the second floor and sit on the enclosed back porch. I storm out, as if I was mad because I can't find my cigarettes. He lets me out and locks the door. I come back a few minutes later so that my friend could come downstairs to let me in. We tip toed back up to the second-floor back porch and stayed there until the action began. Sure enough this plan worked. We're on the second floor for about an hour tops. Then we hear the girls come in. We don't run down immediately, we are waiting for the perfect timing. We are upstairs, they are downstairs drinking and having a good ole time. This last about another hour, we finally hear one of the guys yell out, he wants the girls to get naked. OK, so that was our cue for action so we ran downstairs and busted them all. One of the guys was so mad at us, he grabbed a can of raid and lighter and made a torch. He was so mad we had messed up his action.

The crazy part is after this night, the women that were there, explained how they wanted to meet us. Two of them had originally started talking to Fred and my friends' boyfriend, but they were getting caught up so much that they told the girls about us. We ended up befriending the young ladies. But once again the madness didn't stop there

The following year, one of the guys and my boyfriend Fred decided to move together on the 1st floor of the building where we hung out. I was there almost every day, if not every day. With the constant cheating, you would have thought that I would be fed up by now, but all I was thinking, he was all Keke known truly as a father, so I wasn't giving up without a fight. It wasn't a fight, but I nearly lost my life and didn't know what was even about to go down until years after the event.

 Here is another episode of the cheating but the method this time was different. Fred would start an argument with me and it would escalate and his friend would come and tell me I had to go because it was getting to heated and come back tomorrow. I noticed one night, Fred left me in the room sleep and it was some different ladies over to his house. Fred was in the Living room with these ladies so I called him into the bedroom, and asked him, what was up with that scenario. Well we argued and Fred ended up walking me home that night. The girls were still at his house, but he stayed with me on my porch a little while to kind of smooth things over. The next day I go over there and these same women are there still. She is giving me all kinds of nasty look, so I look at Fred, and sarcastically I say "Oh, so I guess you plan on sending me home again tonight." He looked at me and was said, "No!"

 Me and Fred were enjoying one another's company, having a good time, we end our evening in his bedroom. A few hours later someone is banging at the door. I tried to get up, because I know it's the girl. I had watched her demeanor all night and I knew something went down between her and Fred. What woman would act in such a manner and nothing is going on between them. Plus, I hear a woman voice and its sounds like hers. But Fred grabs, me and tells me "I got it." He opens the door and as she tries to walk in, he pushed her out and closes the door behind him. As I am tugging on the door, he is holding the knob and after a few tugs on the knob he finally let go of the door, but when I opened the door, their conversation was over. I saw her walking away, as he was pushing me back into the room. I didn't even have to ask what that was all about, but tell you about the stupidity in myself, I thought I was somebody special cause he made her go find some business that night. BUT! He made me go find some business the night before when she was over there. He was just with her the night before. Silly ME!!

I found out years later through my friend Keisha that this young lady was planning to stab me. Keisha told me she showed up at the house with her guy later that night. This is something I did not know because I was in the room with Fred I didn't even know Keisha had even showed up that night. Keisha told me, when she walked up to the building the girl was on the front porch sharpening her knife, and told them how she was about to cut this girl up that was in the house. My friend said at first, she didn't know the woman was talking about, until she got a little more information from her. Keisha said, once she caught on to who she was talking about (me), Keisha allowed her to finish her rant. Keisha said once she was all done sharpening her knife, she began to walk toward Fred's room. Keisha said she walked behind her, because she was also ready for battle if she was about to even make good on her plan to stab me. First of all, this was over a guy, who wasn't claiming her. She had been over there twice and she was ready to lock him down. I think about how a relationship that wasn't God ordained almost cost me my life, I didn't even know, it was God's protection and grace that kept me safe that night. The plan the enemy had against my life that night I found out about years later, so when you talk about grace and mercy, I picture this moment in my life.

The devil had a hit out on my life from the beginning. I bet he thought he was going to succeed that night. I look back and I began to think about how my bad decision and insecurities allowed me to stay in this relationship. He cheated on me so many times and I felt like if I fought and stayed and showed him I would be down for him, that Fred would see that and he would become faithful.

Chapter Eight

I Da Pappy[4] Boss

As I said in the previous chapter, I tried to stay with Fred to show my loyalty in hopes that things would change. I mean all the work I put in, he had to have changed, right? So far from the truth. Well things did not change, I wanted to get him back for cheating on me so many times. I stepped out on him and started to spend time with other guys. I did this for about a good year. Some I was intimate with, some I wasn't. Let me tell you about the ones I was intimate with.

The first guy I was intimate with, I met while me and my girls were hanging out. I don't remember where we were exactly, because we weren't always at a party. We liked to eat, so I am sure we were at a restaurant or something, but anyway. I meet this guy. He seemed nice, but I didn't really like him because I never really liked guys that were drug dealers, so I wasn't taking him serious at all. It was my birthday weekend and I decided to hang out with him. I didn't want it to just be him and me as I said I wasn't really feeling this guy, so I asked if he had some friends and we could make it a group outing. We decided we would go hang out on the North side of Chicago and him and his friends rented a hotel room. We were drinking alcohol, they had weed (I smoked weed once in my life, found out that wasn't for me. Felt like I was walking through life in slow motion, never did that again). Drinking alters

---

[4] Life. Dir. Ted Demme. Movie. 1999.

your thinking and feelings, but one thing led to another and I ended up in the bed with this guy. Strange thing, we ended up in the room alone. It's still fuzzy how I ended up alone in the room with this dude. I thought my friends left me there, but I called one of them who had a cell phone and asked them, where they were? They told me they went to get something to eat, so I told them to please hurry and come get me. By this time, I am sobering up, mad at myself for even being in this position. When they got there, I didn't wake him up, I didn't say good-bye, I just left.

He tried calling me, I either ignored his calls or just pulled every spin move I could, just to get him to leave me alone. My excuses were, I had something to do, or no baby sitter was available. After a while he caught my drift and I never heard from him again.

2 weeks after he stopped calling me. Once again me and the girls were hanging out as usual over the weekend, we went out after dinner we came back to the neighborhood park to hang out and we bumped into some guys we went to elementary school with. They were from the neighborhood and we knew them, or should I say we knew of them. There was a group of us, but two of the guys asked if me and one of my other friends would hang out with them for the remainder of the evening. We accepted the invitation and went with these 2 guys. While riding around drinking we ended up at the hotel. I ended up in the bed with this guy. The crazy part is I did really like this guy. We even hung out the next day, before he went back to school. After gaining interest in this guy, I didn't go hang out with Fred anymore. I went over and hung out with my friends, but I began to distance myself from

Fred. This new guy name was Calvin.

After about a week, Calvin and I decided to become official and call us a couple. About another week and a half later, I had a scheduled doctor's appointment to get my Depo Provera shot. When I got to the clinic they did a pregnancy test and I found out I was pregnant. Once again, the doctor does a pelvic exam and says I am about 2 weeks pregnant. So before I leave the office, I have to tell the doctor about my current life style. I told her about the guy who I was with for my birthday weekend, but I came on my menstruation 3 days after my birthday, (Being a woman you know to calculate or mark the first date of your last period, so that you are aware and not caught off guard by your period the following month and this particular date is fresh in my head because of the confusion I had about who the father was and it was always easy to remember because it was my brother Jeff's birthday) so the doctor told me to eliminate him. Then I told her about Fred and Calvin. I had sex with Fred 1 week before I had sex with Calvin. She eliminated Fred because of the size of my uterus and potential ovulation dates. Which left me with Calvin. Now I have to call this guy who is away at college, and inform him that he has a baby on the way.

I called one of my friends, for moral support just in case he flipped out on me when I told him, I would have a shoulder to cry on. But Calvin didn't flip out at all, he seemed happy. I explained to Calvin about me and Fred being in a relationship and how the doctor said it could only be him. He wanted to go with me to my first doctors' appointment. When we went, I had the doctor explain the scenario to him as well. As time went on, I would go to visit him in school and he would come home on weekends and we would hang out at his house but the distance drove a wedge between Calvin and me. It was Valentine's Day weekend, and Calvin was supposed to pick me up for the weekend but he wasn't answering any of my calls. I was really broken this weekend. I was so hurt I had to get out the house. I left all types of nasty voicemails on his answering machine. He called me the next day and broke up with me, but I found out later he spent Valentine's Day with another young lady.

I went through the rest of the pregnancy alone. Calvin would call me from time to time and check on me, ask me about the doctor appointments, he would even give me money here and there, but I was single with another baby daddy.

When Fred found out I was pregnant, he didn't say anything to me at all. Now I would still go over there to hang out with my friends, but I wasn't hanging with Fred my whole pregnancy. My friends would ask me if I was sure that wasn't Fred's baby. I gave them the scenario between me and Calvin and how the doctor eliminated Fred. Their doubts made me feel like Calvin may have some doubts as well.

My friends decided to throw me a baby shower. Actually, it was one of Fred's best friend whom he shared the apartment with idea. I also made him this babies Godfather. They threw me a great baby shower that shocked everyone. My grandmother even believed the baby shower wasn't going to turn out the way we expected, but it turned out better. My grandmother would say, "Watch, you have to come out of your own pocket for that party." Well they pulled it off. Decorations were nice, one of our other guy's BBQed, Ms. Edna made my Taffy apple salad, and I had amazing gifts and a huge cake from Roser's bakery. I invited Calvin's family, but they didn't show up. Only his sister secretly stopped by. I love that girl. No matter what, she shows genuine love for me, even to this very day. But everything turned out wonderful.

Calvin came over later that night to check out the gifts, I must say I believe he was surprised as well to see that it turned out as good as it did. Out of Loneliness I went with him to his God Parents house and spent the night with him. I know I shouldn't have but loneliness can make you be in the most broken situations.

Time to have the baby!!

It was July 9th, and I woke up early in the morning. No pain just walking around, but my grandmother was up ironing her clothes for work. She took one look at me and said, "I'm not going to work. You're having that baby today." I told her I wasn't in any pain. But she insisted she'd stay home, I told her "OK, but I don't think I will have the baby today." My grandmother called my auntie and told her to take her to the job to fill out leave of absence papers. While they were gone, I decided to get in the shower. When I stepped in the shower, I had pain out of this world that shot from my back to my stomach. When they came back home, my grandmother looked at me and asked me, if I were ready to go to the hospital yet. I told her that I was ready, but she went to the kitchen and pulled out some lunch meat, mayo and bread. She sat at the table and began to put Mayo on her bread. By the way, she was moving in a slow artistic motion with the butter knife as she spread the Mayo on the bread. I gave her a look like "Come On!"

And she looked at me and said, "Oh you seriously ready to go now." I said yes. She called my mom and told her, "Meet us at the hospital, it's time to have a baby."

As my aunt Sharon drove us to the hospital, this labor was moving fast. With every contraction, I could literally feel my cervix open. The weirdest thing I ever felt in my life. I get to the hospital and when the nurse did my pelvic exam I was 7 centimeters. Now you know I am smiling, because I realize this is almost over and I am not in excruciating pain. But my grandmother looks and me and notice that I am smiling, she says, "Stop smiling or they won't help you." I put this painful look on my face, just to satisfy her. They put me in the room and shortly after that Calvin walks in. 30 minutes (quickest and easiest labor I ever had) later I have a baby girl. I named her Dacia Janee Diamond. I chose Dacia because it means "Purple flower" in African. Purple is my favorite color and she was precious to me. My oldest daughter Keke named her Diamond. Keke would literally rub my belly the whole time I was pregnant and say, "Hey Diamond." and Calvin named her Janee. But once labor was over and everybody was out of the room and it was nobody but me and Calvin, I asked him if he wanted a DNA test. He told me, "No." I asked if he was sure and he said, "Yes." I left it alone from there.

Chapter Nine

Minnesota Nice

After having Dacia, me and Calvin tried again to make our relationship work, for the sake of Dacia, but I knew him too well. I knew when he was cheating without any evidence at all. We didn't last long at all. To make matters worse. The day after we broke up, he brought this young lady with him to pick up my baby. How I found out? I walked on the porch as he was getting Dacia ready to go with him and I look in his car and there is a strange lady, I have never seen and she is waving at me. Of course, I didn't wave back. I turn around go back in the house and slapped the stew out of Calvin. Okay, Okay, I know I was wrong for putting my hands on him, but I was hurt to my soul with that one. It just let me know, how he really felt about me.

A short while after that, me and Fred got back together. I remember the night we began talking again, he saw me at Kells Park. Calvin was at my house watching Dacia for me. He was only there to give me a break so that I can go and hang out. Fred took one look at me and said, "There goes wifey!" I turned around to see if it was someone was behind me but it wasn't. He came and hugged me. Now allow me to remind you this man had not said anything to me since the pregnancy began, even after I had the baby. He asked me if I was hungry. I told him yes. It was late, so we went to Best Sub restaurant on Chicago Ave. When we walked in we saw Calvin's friend Marcell. Now this guy saw me with Fred, but I spoke like all was well, because truthfully it was.

Marcell asked me where Calvin was, and I told Marcell he was at my house. Of course, Marcell called Calvin and told Calvin where I was and who I was with. After me and Fred ate and talked we went back to Fred's house and honestly, I can't remember if we did more than just talked that night, but we decided to get back together. I went home fairly close to morning. Calvin was upset, but I didn't care. He brought a woman to my house and you're mad cause I am out with a man and we are not together? I told him, WHATEVER! And meant that with my whole heart.

After me and Fred got back together, he even accepted Dacia wholeheartedly. What he did for Keke, he did for Dacia. He did not separate the 2. His heart was and still is genuine when it comes down to these girls.

I began to feel empty, I wasn't doing hair anymore unless it was at my house. I felt the shop life was way too busy for me, because I couldn't spend enough time with my children. I decided to go back to school and chose Robert Morris for Medical Assistant; graduated in 2002 but couldn't find a job for 6 months. Spent all this money for school, student loans and nobody wanted to hire me at entry level. Now most people were getting hired at their internship. Not me, I was being sexually harassed by the doctor, and I wasn't giving in. As time was winding down, I knew this doctor was going to give me a bad review because he started to treat me, cold. So, I told my school about it and they found me another clinic to complete my hours of internship. These hours are needed to graduate and take the certification. Where they sent me was last minute and they were not hiring any newbies at the time. When I left that first clinic where I was being sexually harassed, one older lady who worked there looked at me said, "I already know why you're leaving, you don't even have to tell me." She told me I was doing the right thing, by leaving.

Things were hard for me, and I had a talk with my Aunt Ingrid, and explained to her that I couldn't find a job. She was staying in Minneapolis, Minnesota. My Aunt told me to come there and life would change for me. I left Chicago and went to Minnesota. I had to stay in the shelter for a couple months, until I got on my feet. Within a week in Minnesota I had a job, and I was able to stack my money and get my first very own apartment. The day I got my apartment Fred came to visit me in Minnesota, but that visit turned into a permanent stay.

At first all was well. Fred went and got a job and he would bring me the check saying, "Leave him a small amount." Fred was happy to leave Chicago. In Chicago, his life was spiraling downward as he was hanging with the wrong people and he was always drunk and high. But Minnesota changed him, at least for a little while.

Like I say, we were doing well. We even had a system for daycare, He would drop them off, and I would pick them up. The evenings he had off, he would pick the kids up early, do homework and cook dinner so I could come home and kick my feet up. We had it made. Then Dacia began having problems at daycare. She had a terrible habit of biting kids. The daycare would call me and tell saying, "If she does this again, you will have to come get her from school." Fred couldn't because his job wasn't stationary, he had to make deliveries around the city and surrounding areas. So, Dacia's biting habit would not stop. I would have to pick her up from the daycare. This got so bad, that my job had to let me go. I found another daycare and looked for a job. I found a job and Dacia habit started all over again, so I got fired from that job as well. After this I made the decision to work for a temp agency, so I wouldn't have to worry about being fired again and I also got a second job at "Super Cuts" doing hair.

In 2003, I became pregnant with my 3rd child. Yes, I am on child number 3 with 3 different men. Fred and I had already been together so many years and I thought we had been through the worst. I had a baby on him and never did he ever throw that in my face. It was almost as if it never happened. He blamed himself for the breach in our relationship. Even though he felt this way it did not stop him from cheating when we relocated to Minnesota. I found out he was getting really acquainted with a lady at one of the stores he would deliver products to. So here I am, hurt yet again.

I had my 3rd child on November 5th, which is the same day as Fred's birthday. We named her Tiffany. After the birth of the baby things took a turn for the worse. Fred had begun hanging with the wrong people, now in Minnesota. It started off with my Uncle Rick when he first moved to Minnesota, then after a while, Fred accumulated more associates. The relationship with these people resulted in Fred losing his job and ultimately his family. Fred, My Uncle and their other counterparts were doing drugs. Fred tried to hide it from me, but he couldn't. I grew up with addicts in my house, so I know the signs. I would ask my Aunt Ingrid, what was going on and if Fred was getting high. I just wanted her to say no really. She would never flat out say yes though. She would speak in parables and I knew then, because my auntie has always been straightforward with me, so by her speaking in riddles I just knew Fred had been getting high too.

I to asked Fred if he was getting high, and with a straight face he denied it of course. I even told him I would stay with him if he was, and be of support if he would agree to get some help. Then I told him I would leave him if I find out he's getting high. He told me, if he was getting high, he wouldn't blame me for leaving, because he wouldn't want his daughters seeing him like that. Eventually I found out the truth, when Fred first lost his job, we began to struggle a bit. We were running low on food so we would go to the food shelters, but that wasn't enough. We were waiting on Fred's very last check after his termination. During this time, we both were using my bank account for direct deposit. I checked the balance often, so one day I checked and it had some available funds. I then went to Fred and told him I think his last check was deposited. He looked at me and said, "I don't think so." I looked at him and said, "It had to, since it is not payday for me."

I called my next-door neighbors, who became like family to us and they would take us wherever we needed to go. I asked them to take me to the grocery store. When they picked me up we stopped at a corner store and while we were there, my neighbor Denise told me to buy something to make sure the money was on the card. I believe she did this because she picked up on the uncertainty in Fred's voice when I said his check was in the bank. When I tried to purchase something, my card was declined. I asked the cashier to check it again. It declined a second time. So now I am in a state of confusion and I check my bank account again, and it gave me the same exact balance it gave me earlier. My neighbor then told me to call the bank and find out what's going on.

I called the bank and they told me, someone had been depositing blank checks and then they tried to withdraw. Then informed me they had pictures from the ATM and asked me if I would come in to the branch to see if I can identify the person. I called Fred and explained to him what was going on with the bank account, and he didn't say much, but I could tell he knew something about it. When I got to the bank, I explained to the teller why I was there and they escorted me to a room in the back of the bank. The Banker showed me some pictures and sure enough, it was Fred and his friend in the pictures. They were showing him deposit empty envelopes and trying to withdraw cash. The Banker asked me, if I knew who that was. I lied and said "NO!" They canceled my card and ordered me another one.

I got home and I was mad as I could have ever been. I had to think about how I was about to deal with this so I came in and just sat on the couch - I just gave Fred a look. He instantly started explaining to me, that it was he and how sorry he was. I was so angry I couldn't say anything at all, I just let him talk. I know I would have said something so hurtful to him. Fred was depositing emptying envelops in the bank to try to withdraw money. Hurtful and embarrassing situation, now I was beginning to be fed up.

And to only make matters worse, Fred began to spend nights away from home. He didn't have a cell phone anymore, so I had no way to get in touch with him when he did this. I remember one night he was out, and he left with my bankcard unbeknownst to me. This time it was money in the bank. I began to check my card and I saw some money had been taken out of the account. I checked it again an hour later and more money was coming out of the account. I kept checking it and as I checked the bank account was getting lower and lower. I began to cry, I had no way to get to him so that I could get my card back. This was the last straw, I was so fed up and tired. A few days later we got into an argument because I said something to my uncle. You hear me, I said we got into an argument cause I something to MY UNCLE. Fred jumped in me and my uncle's disagreement and I told him I was tired, done, and he needed to leave.

After Fred left I will be honest, I felt as if a burden was removed. The crazy part is my Aunt and Uncle allowed him to stay with them. I began to realize that the women in my family feel as if a man is needed. I remember my Grandmother told me I needed to let Fred come back, because I got these babies, and who else is going to help me with these babies? So, every chance they got they tried to talk me into letting him come back. I was not breaking down. It was like a tug of war with my family and my happiness. I remember I thought the only person I could talk to that made sense was my mother - until I was told that even my Mom was saying that I should let Fred come home. I began to feel like my Mom was playing both sides. Saying one thing when she was with me and then saying another when she was with my Aunt and Grandmother.

After all this madness, I decided to move back to Chicago after few months, I had to get away. I began to get away on weekends and escape to Chicago to spend time with my cousin Dondrell as well as get things together for my move back. While I was hanging with him, he played matchmaker and introduced me to his friend and we began dating. One weekend I even invited this guy to my house in Minnesota.

I wrote previously where I explained my biological father made plans to come back to Minnesota with me, but never showed up to the Greyhound bus station. Around this time is when that occurrence happened, so during this time I was dealing with a lot, and it caused me to make some bad decisions. Man after man. Feeling rejected, unloved and lost.

A broken soul can cause us to make irrational decisions. Ones that cause destruction. Satan was after my life and these were direct avenues for him to take hold, through relationships. Hurt people, hurt people.

Although I thought I was a strong black woman for leaving one man, I was fearful of being alone, so I didn't wait on healing and I began to take my hurt and insecurities with me, everywhere I went and wore it with whomever I was with.

Chapter Ten

Back to Chicago

I made the move back to my hometown Chicago in 2004. Back to familiarity. My sister's mother told me I could rent her place. She had section 8 vouchers but wasn't utilizing the apartment, so she co-leased it to me for the amount she was to pay section 8, which was $150. She knew it would be awhile before I would get any cash, and she told me I could pay her in stamps until I get the cash. I was looking for work and my sister's mom was also assisting me with my search for employment as well. The first month there I get emergency food stamps and I call her right away and give her the card, I still had not received my cash assistance because they were still approving it. Oh, yes and I paid her to move in as well. Now my boyfriend at the time was the guy that my cousin Dondrell introduced me to. He was helping me a lot with cash during the time that I was not receiving cash assistance. He also made sure my hair was done for interviews, brought clothes and paid my phone bill. Now he was spending a lot of time with me, at the apartment I was renting, even though he had his own apartment.

Shortly after I moved in to the apartment, she had her son and his fiancée to move in with me. I was still paying her in food stamps when her son and fiancée moved in. After a couple months, I finally receive cash assistance. The same day I got my cash, I went and got some stuff for the house, and paid my own phone bill for that month. That first month I had only received

$100 in cash because it was based upon the income I received those last 2 months I was in Minnesota that I had employment. I get home from paying my phone bill and my sisters Mother is there. She looks at me, and tells me she came to get the cash off the card. First off I had just given her over $150 in food stamps, so I couldn't understand why she wanted the cash too. Secondly how did she find out I had money on my card? Let me tell you, she wrote down the link card information and was checking my link account daily.

After telling her what I had just spent the money on, because I didn't think I should give her my cash, because I had just given her food stamps to cover that month's rent, she looked at me and told me to get out of her apartment; don't wait until later, get all my stuff out at that very moment. She was also upset because my boyfriend was there a lot. She was upset because my boyfriend was there often but her son and his fiancée had moved in and that was not a part of the deal. But without too much back and forth I gave her the apartment back. Ultimately, I had to move into my boyfriend's apartment. Since my cousin had a huge van, we could move out of her apartment in only a few trips.

Moving in with my boyfriend was not what I had in mind. His mother owned a duplex on the West side of Chicago. She stayed on the first floor and my boyfriend stayed on the second floor. Now, I was unemployed so my boyfriend took care of all the bills, rent and whatever we needed. I enrolled in classes at Kennedy King College, to finish prerequisites for Nursing. Then I got hired on as a casual working at the post office. My boyfriend had 2 kids himself, that would come over on the weekends.

Eventually, my boyfriend's EX dropped the kids off and never picked them back up because she was upset that about me and my kids moving into his apartment, so in her mind she was trying to make things hard for us. It wasn't like he was a deadbeat father; this man took care of his kids. While they were with us, whatever I did for my children, I did for his and vice versa. Now we are living in a 3-bedroom house with 5 children. My boyfriend's mother had a daycare and she became caretaker to all the kids. Childcare assistance was compensating her for my three daughters, but my boyfriend had to pay out-of-pocket for his two sons. Yet, we are still making things happen, we are even planning to get married at this point.

    Shortly after we hit a few massive bumps and my boyfriend's job completely shut down so now he and my cousin Dondrell were out of work. Then shortly after that, my casual position at the post office was over, and I had to reapply, but the hours they assigned me were conflicting with my school hours. I had to quit school to make sure we had enough, financially, to have our needs met. My boyfriend was having a hard time finding employment, so he would watch the kids, while his mother would still get paid through childcare assistance. Those payments would cover rent, or if he had an interview or something to do, she would be paid to watch the kids. My boyfriend began hang out with his Cousin and that wasn't a good sign. The reason this was uncomfortable for me is because I knew family lived a life headed for destruction. I told my boyfriend beforehand, I don't deal with men who sell drugs and that it was a deal breaker for me and I would have to say good bye to him. He began to come home with money although it wasn't much, it may have been what some would call "two's and few's," but now I begin to wonder what is going on. I asked him, "Where is this money coming from?" He said, "My Cousin." OK, so the first few times I didn't find it too suspect, because I know him and his cousin has helped one another a lot. Then it began to seem as if every day he had some money.

I kept asking him where was the cash coming from and why would his cousin continue giving him money daily for no apparent reason. Then I noticed he would go over there at the same time every day as if he was punching in and punching out. Leaving home at the same time every day and coming back home at the same time. I knew then he was attempting to sell drugs, he liked nice things and when he had a drink, it was never anything cheap. As I stated previously, drug dealing is a deal breaker for me. I began to be disgusted at the sight of him, especially since the cash he was bringing home was only enough for some restaurant food, cigarettes, and his alcohol beverage. Now here is a grown man with children at home and you're outside risking your life for pennies.

During this time of my boyfriend's street life adventure, we had another problem that sealed the deal of me leaving him for good. Around Christmas time that year. Childcare assistance had a freeze and wasn't paying providers for a few months. From the time his mother started caring for my children until this freeze, she only received one payment, so I was told. She began requesting money for the first month he was off work so I went to talk to her and she told me while I was at work, that my boyfriend would leave the kids with her on certain days and she would even feed them on days that he was home with them. She said by her using her time to help, those funds would not be taken out for rent. I agreed with that and began to pay her what was owed.

My boyfriend and I, at that point are paying rent out of our pockets, and she continued to watch the children. His mom begins complaining about childcare not paying her, so we had to pay her out-of-pocket. 3 months go by and she is still saying she hasn't received back pay from childcare yet. Still young, naive and thinking that I could trust her I went along with that, and we still paid her for childcare.

My oldest daughter Keke's God Father Wayne comes to pick me up to take me to handle some business and we get to their house and I explain the issue of childcare not paying my boyfriend's mother and that didn't sit right in him or his wife's spirits, so they helped me call childcare assistance and I found out she had been paid and her payments were regular. I was so livid when I got home, I went straight to my boyfriend and showed him the payment history. Now, we are paying out of our pockets childcare, and rent so this means his mother is getting double childcare I am paying her out of my pocket and we are paying rent. As I gave it to my boyfriend he just looked at it, then I said, "Well what are you going to do?" He looked at me and said, "What am I supposed to do, go downstairs and slap her!" I gave him one of the nastiest look I could give a person and I said, "NO, but you need to say something." Then he said he would address the issue.

The next day when I get home from work, I asked my boyfriend did he talk with his mother about the checks. He told me "No, not yet." That made me angrier than I was the day before. I didn't say anything right then and there because I was too mad and didn't know how to approach this or what to think about my boyfriend. Suddenly, his mother calls my cell phone and, her conversation start off with a chuckle and she says, "Did my son tell you what I told him today?" I said, "No." She proceeded and said, "I told him when I do start getting the checks I'm gonna only give him like $10 dollars out of it, but I was just playing and he got so mad." She began chuckling again. You ever seen the cartoons where they have smoke comes from their ears, well, that was me. I was taught to respect my elders, so I told his mother to let me call her back. I went to the bedroom where my boyfriend was and I went completely off the handle. He had just told me he had not talked to his mother regarding the checks, but when she brought up the checks, was that not the perfect opportunity to say anything? I know they heard me going off, the whole block may have heard me, I was so loud. Her bedroom was directly under ours. I snapped so loud just so his mother would hear me.

 Then I told him come on, we are going to talk to her now. At first, he refused to go down there with me because I was angry, but after a little more of me snapping and acting irrational, we finally went downstairs to speak with his mother. When we made it to the front door of her house she already knew what this meeting was about. She now owed US some money. But when we sat down with her and I told her the days she got paid and the amount. She looked me dead in the face and said, "What was I supposed to do, it was Christmas time and I wanted to get some nice things for my kids." Now my boyfriend is sitting beside me not opening his mouth. Then she made a statement that she had been giving my boyfriend money. At this point the only logic I could make of this was that mother and son was in on this whole thing together. He had to have known about this money.

I told his mother, "I will be moving out soon and I will live out whatever she owes me. I got rebellious in this situation. I moved my little sister in to his apartment, I didn't pay a bill, and I even began to cheat on him. One guy lived in the neighborhood where we were staying. That didn't last long, I didn't like the guy that much and it was too close to the place we lived

While still making preparation to move out, a male friend that I grew up with, introduced me to one of his friends. I had not told my close friends what had happened, so every time they saw me I was alone. My male friend hooked me up with his friend, because he said, "whenever we go out you are always by yourself, I have a good guy for you." One day while we were all at the neighborhood park, my friend introduced us to this guy. We exchanged numbers and decided we would hook up.

So, I called the guy to see if he wanted to hang out. We hung out for a while, and we eventually ended up at his house. That surely was not what I was about, so I told him to take me home. I explained to him I was in a situation and I wasn't trying to start anything with anybody until I got out of that.

I moved out of my boyfriend mothers building (Ex-boyfriend at that point), and I move into my oldest daughter God Parents basement. My little sister and I were to go half on the $1000 rent. When it got close to rent time my sister didn't have her portion, so I end up, having to make her leave. At this point, all I have is the $500 and now I am in a tight bind. I was in between jobs and I was up for a job at University of Illinois Hospital, but I had not got a call for an interview yet.

At this point I am single, but I am dating 2 guys. One of them is the guy that my male friend introduced me to. I am not really feeling this, so I need to do a process of elimination, so I tell both I am $500 dollars short on my rent. My plan was, the one who helps I will continue to talk to. So, I asked both, but only one-stepped up. This was the guy my male friend hooked me up with. His name was Tyray. We hadn't made our relationship official, but he didn't mind helping me out financially and every weekend became a party at my house. We would invite our close friends to come hang out at my house. We would order a Football pizza, get a fifth of Hennessey and a 24 pack of Corona, our friends over and it was a party.

Even during this foolery, I began to go back to church I grew up in with my oldest daughters Godparents. I had been MIA for a few years, from the time I left for Minnesota until 2006. That was approximately 4 years. After going to a meeting with my daughters God mother Ernesta and the minister there spoke into our lives, something clicked but at this point, that click wasn't hard enough to make me go full-fledged onto the right path. But I began to pick up the bible more. Not daily, but maybe once a week. I remember after that meeting I began to pray to God and ask for this job to come through. Finally, in September 2006 I got an interview for the University of Illinois. I had been doing follow up calls, maybe every 2 days. It was my birthday October 5th, I had received my very last unemployment check, so I prayed and said, "God I don't know what you have planned or if you have anything planned for me, but I hope I get a job real soon, I have 3 little girls to take care of." I called the University and guess what… I was hired! Yes…a job. I praised God that day. Proof that He reigns on the unjust. Because I know I was unjust and shall I say spiritually dead.

During this time, I was a lost soul and was tormented by lust and generational curses. I gave my body away; my attitude was terrible and I hurt people. I did things without remorse. I was full of unforgiveness as well as bitterness. I had a victim mentality, I was perfect and everybody else was messed up. I couldn't find a fault in myself, everyone else had the problem. Truth is I had problems myself. Much insecurity, used sex and relationships as a way of escape, fearful, lonely, you name it. I was a hot commodity for hell, a child of disobedience. Everywhere the enemy saw an opening, I let him in to have full reign.

Chapter Eleven

Two Broken People Won't Make a Whole

Single, strong, black, working woman of three children is what I called myself. Tyray and I become an official couple, but there was no trust. We started off all wrong and even before we made it official I had become sexually active with him. He was dealing with other women and I competed for the title. We were also practicing unprotected sex, and we ended up with an STD. Thank God it was something I could get rid of. I told Tyray and we went to the doctor for his medication. He believed he knew who he contracted the disease from so I asked him did he tell the women he was with. He informed me, that he had, and this was when him and me became an official couple.

    We may have made it official but, the cheating did not stop there. One night Tyray came to my house late, but we both had to get up and go to work that next morning. He always got up significantly earlier than I. Yet, this morning I got up out of the bed while Tyray was in the shower and when I walked out of the kitchen, there was a condom on the ironing board. We were not using condoms, still even after the incident. I got very angry and told him to get out and we broke up that day. He later called and apologized and I fell for the oke doke. I began to check his phone and his voicemail.

    One day we had company over we were drinking and his phone kept ringing, but he wouldn't answer it. So, I said, "That can't be anybody but that whore!" Tyray looked at me and said,

"But she is MY whore!" Lord, why'd he say that?! Now I will be the first to admit that I swung first. I hauled off and slapped the mess out of Tyray. He got up, grabbed me around my neck, the chair falls back with me in it. He begins to choke me and dig his nails into my neck. His little brother who was there with us, comes and grabs him off me. His brother's girlfriend is also there and she helps me up off the floor. Tyray tells his brother, he is tired of me and comes over where I am and begins to muff my head into the wall, repeatedly while calling me names and cursing me out. My daughters Godparents come running down to the basement because they can hear what is happening. They calmed us down, and set us in separate rooms to talk to us. We decided not to break up, the next morning we apologized to one another and went on about life as if nothing happened.

  A few weeks later I was at work and received a call from my second daughter's dad Calvin. He tells me, "I took a test and Dacia is not my daughter." I was literally frozen, in a complete state of confusion for 2 reasons. I was told by the doctor that Calvin was the only possible man, or this had to be some sick joke, because I asked him did he want to take a test as soon as she was born and now he waits until she is 5 years old and then don't tell me, He does it behind my back? That is not the type of friendship Calvin and I had, I mean we talk about so much stuff. We would discuss each other's relationship together, whatever problems we were facing, I mean Calvin had literally become an amazing friend. I felt if this is what he wanted to do, we could have done this together. I am in front of my co-workers and can't really say what I want to say, so I tell him to let me call him back in a few minutes. I go outside the building because anxiety has kicked in, I'm sweating and everything.

    I began to ask Calvin how and why? He told because he wanted to try to get custody of Dacia and wanted legal proof to get her from me. He said they did an at home DNA test. At that time, my oldest Keke and Dacia were going over their house every day because they were going to a charter school that Calvin enrolled them in. I went to go pick the girls up from Calvin house and he passes me this DNA paper that says Dacia is not his daughter. So, I go home and I am explaining what happened to Keke's Godparents and Keke interjects and says, "Mommy I think I remember when they did that." I asked her what happened and she began to explain. Calvin and his wife were not married at the time this happened, but she was the one who performed the test. So Keke said that when it was Dacia's turn to be swabbed Calvin's girlfriend pushed him out of the bathroom and closed the door. My daughter Keke said she asked Calvin's girlfriends daughter what was going on. She is a couple years younger than my daughter, but she knew what was going on. She told my daughter, they were taking a test to see if Dacia was really Calvin's child. My daughter said she told their daughter that she was going to tell me, and the little girl told my daughter, "Go ahead my momma, not scared of your momma!" I asked my daughter why she didn't tell me, but Keke told me, she didn't want to have me and Tinika arguing. My kids liked going over there.

    Of course, I called and snapped and said, "maybe your girlfriend swabbed her own mouth, if she threw you out the bathroom while she swabbed Dacia. I mean I went off on both." I felt more betrayed by Calvin because we could have taken care of this from the beginning, then the fact he was trying to take my baby from me. After the fighting calmed down, Calvin and I talked and he decided he didn't want Dacia to know about this, he is continuing life as her dad. I asked was he positive that this was what he wanted to do. He said how he loved Dacia and he already had a bond with her and wanted to keep it. So, we went on about life as such

During all the back and forth I told Fred that is a possibility that he was the father of Dacia. He accepted that as such. Honestly Fred had never changed what he did with my kids from day one. When he did for one, he did for the others. This was also a time when Tyray was there for me. He was there through the tears of this, he moved in and things began to be OK with us again. At least for a little while,

Tyray kept on cheating and this caused many more fights. He would curse me out and call me out of my name. It got so bad that I began to curse him and call him out of his name. I thought if I did it back this would stop him. But this only made matters worse. This eventually turned into full-fledged fighting between Tyray and me. We eventually moved out of the basement apartment. The reason we moved, was because the lights were cut off. The bill wasn't paid and it was included in the rent while rent was paid on time. But these people were family, it was Keke's Godparents. The one thing I hate about this whole deal with me moving is that I turned on them when they never turned their back on me. I look back on that now and I look at how they have always been there for me, even after that. Keke's Godmother who I call my sister, never said one bad thing about me, and she forgave me. I am truly sorry left and I up when they were going through a tough time.

When Tyray and me moved into this new apartment, the fighting got worse. One time he came home from work angry and just started fighting me. I ended up on the floor with his foot in my back. The next day, I got up and left the house, didn't say a word to him. He was calling my phone but I wouldn't answer. I didn't want to talk, I wanted him gone. When I got home later he was, crying and saying how mad at himself he was and again I forgave him.

Confession: In 2007 when Tyray and me were together, whenever we would break up, usually for the same thing, I had someone I would spend time with. But when him and me would get back together I would break it off with this guy. I met this guy through my sister. We both were being mistreated and being cheated on so we felt we should occupy our time. Now we didn't plan for it to be a relationship, just something to do when our relationship seemed a little rocky. Now on my end, things did go a little too far and I ended up giving myself to this guy. This guy and me never made it anywhere though, because I had Tyray and then he found a woman and we just put a stop to everything. I never told Tyray this while we were together, not because I was fearful of losing him, but because I hated being belittled. He already called me names when he didn't know what I was doing, so I always worried about how much worse it would be, had I been honest about this. Then all he did was lie and cheat on me, so I felt I did not have to say anything. But now I am putting an end to shame and no longer must I worry about what anyone says or would say about me. The old me, has passed away. I am made a new in Christ, and this can be a testimony for you too! Confess your sins one to another and be forgiven. Bringing light to the darkness and expose the enemy and be free!!

    The first time I had to call the police on him, I went out to hang with some of our friends while he was at work. He called my phone and asked me where was I at. I treated him just like he would treat me, when I would call him. Just gave him all that attitude back, plus I told him I was dancing on a pole. Didn't think he would take me in a literal sense. But he did. We got into an argument and I ended up drunk and couldn't drive home, so I allowed one of the sober people to drive the car. That was my friend Keisha's brother. Two of my friends stayed at my house with me, but we got up early and went to get something to eat. Tyray didn't come home that night, but he came home while I was gone. One of the security doors was looked and he couldn't get in. He called my phone and said, "B**** come open the door right now!" I said sarcastically, "sorry I'm not at home." He said I better get there right now or else. Of course, I wasn't going home to that. Tyray found out from a mutual friend where I was. While I was at my friend's house, Tyray called my phone again, and called me some more vulgar names and then said, "You think this is a game? Go look at your car!!" I just knew he didn't touch my car, because he wouldn't want anybody to touch his car. But that was so far from reality, I went to my car and found my window busted driver side mirror was broken. My friend was ready to go and bust his car windows out. I wasn't going to play this game with Tyray, so I called the police. Later that day I went home and saw he had trashed the whole apartment. My Televisions were turned over on the floors, Ice cream was smeared all over the kitchen floor and he had taken all the food out of the house. He knew I was about to put him out so he asked me to give all his belongings to his friends. Of course, that was a terrible idea, because as soon as we pulled up to my house Tyray pulled up shortly after. I jumped in my friend Keisha's car so he wouldn't get to me.

Tyray's defense was that because I let Keisha's brother drive my car, it had to be something going on between us. That was so far from the truth, he is like a little brother to me. I got a restraining order against Tyray, because this time it had gone a little too far. Once again Tyray charmed me into coming back. He paid for my window and side mirror, then we went to court together and I dropped the restraining order.

In 2008, I became pregnant. This pregnancy was harder than any other pregnancy I had. I was ill and slept majority of the day. That part I could deal with, but my trust issues, rejection, and control spirit was another. One day I checked his voicemail and found out he had a young lady coming to see him at his mother's house. I called him while he was at work and told him exactly what I knew, and I told him I wanted him out. He tried to beg me to stay, but I was so hurt, that he would do this while I was pregnant. I cried myself to sleep, but I woke up the next day with the worst back pain I had ever experienced. I went to work still, in pain and all. I was in more pain at work, then during lunch I went to the bathroom and I began to bleed. I called my doctor and got some blood test done. She told me to wait until the following week and she would draw more blood to check HCG levels. See, this is how they check to make sure you are truly having a miscarriage. She told me, it wasn't a good sign and to try to stay comfortable during the weekend. But that night I was still hurting and bleeding. I tried calling Tyray, but I was not getting an answer because he was sleeping.

I called my Auntie Sharon and told her what was going on and I wanted to just end it, and how do I go about do that. Didn't know if I should go to the hospital, or what. My Aunt is always a jokester, so she said, "I know where you can go, you almost halfway through the process already and laughed. She took me to the abortion clinic and coached me through the process. I informed them I was already losing the baby and that I was in excruciating pain. They weren't the nicest group of people. I should have known this was not of God at that point, I never believed in abortions, but I figured since the baby was already in danger, I just wanted it all to be over and I figured it wouldn't be a big deal, but after the pain was gone and I came to my senses, I began to be tormented. Even though I was already losing the baby, the process of the D&C became a horrible memory for me. I began to think what if that was my baby boy? What if I would have held on one more day., would my baby have made it?

Well, after this we got back together, he seemed remorseful and I felt that I needed the comfort at that point. As always things are good in the beginning, but always short-lived. The doctor would not put me on birth control now, because everything was causing me high blood pressure. I was undecided on getting the IUD, which is a device they plant in your uterus for 5 years. This was the option, because I needed something non-hormonal to keep my blood pressure from spiking up. I was afraid to get this contraceptive, because I had heard many horror stories from this device puncturing your uterine wall to it having to be surgically removed from your uterus if you are not able to find the string attached to make sure it's in place. Well I guess you already know what happened, I became pregnant once again and now it's 2009. This was my 4th child, Serenity born March 2010.

While I was pregnant, the arguing didn't stop. He would say mean things about my kids during the arguments. One statement that was said was, "My child would never turn out like them other 3!!" I would defend my children, but this still had effects on my babies because they heard it. My insecurities and fear of being alone kept me there, plus I would blame it on the alcohol. We always seemed to get along, unless alcohol was involved. Then I would go tit-for-tat with him. He said something about me and the kids, so I would try to say something worse to get under his skin. I mean I would try to go for the jugular. Two wrong does not make a right.

I joined a car club after my 4th child. I felt I needed something to do, especially when Tyray and I were not getting along. I know we hear a lot of things about car clubs, which some are true, but the fact of the matter is if you don't have a whore monger spirit already, the car club won't impart that spirit. I was in the car club and dated no one in the car club. Not to say I wasn't approached. I mean they are social clubs, so you must be social. This group at the time had become more like family. If my car broke down, they were there. If the kids needed anything, they would help. I threw a get together, event, or whatever they made sure they were there to support me. My friend Anjail had a Father's Day party, me and Tyray were not together at the time, but we had mutual friends so Tyray showed up. Now in the mist of the gathering, everyone from the social club were standing together. Still, to this very day have no idea what Tyray thought he saw. But I turned around and Tyray said, "you gone disrespect me like this?" and slapped me. My friend Gina grabbed me, as I tried to pull away from her, I saw Tyray leave the party. I tried to go for the biggest empty bottle I could find to knock him out with it. The social club stopped me, but it didn't stop a few of them from going to their trunks. They just wanted to protect their sister, but I told them, not! But they did stay with me that night to keep me safe. Tyray hated me being in the car club, but wouldn't say that. He felt it made him look like a punk as he would say. So rather than saying that at first, he just would lash out whenever I had a social club outing.

    I know it is stereotypical to be called a slut OR any other vulgar name to have 4 kids and 4 different fathers. To have more than one kid, and have multiple fathers at all, you are degraded, but until we know someone's story or what they were plagued with, how can you judge. One child I made a mistake with, by trying to repay someone for cheating on me and ended up hurting an innocent child, but all my other kids fathers I was with them for years, trying to make something out of nothing. We tend to look for love in all the wrong places, or we as women sometimes believe that if we give a man sex that it changes the dynamics. Which it does, just not in the aspect that we hope for. To most men, not all, but most, sex is just sex. I will admit I thought that sex would make my male counterpart and me closer. Yet, it only complicated things and an ungodly soul tie was created.

Sometimes we stick through relationships, because we feel this is our last chance at love. Especially me, when I got with Tyray my self-esteem was so low, I felt who else would want me, and I have 3 children with 3 different fathers. I listen to the words of my Grandmother when she said, "Who else is going to help you with these 3 kids." This was said when I left Fred. I also listened to the evil statements that were made by people about having babies with multiple fathers. So much so, that I would lie and say the last 3 kids were my husbands or I would say that the first 3 were all Fred's; which is pretty much the truth. He still raised these first three as his own. Whatever he does for Tiffany, he does for Dacia. He also does everything for my oldest and her newborn son. These lies would be to my co-workers, people that were associated with the social clubs or people I just met. Shame of my past had a hold on me. I would worry about what people would say about me, behind my back and to my face honestly. I feared that I would never find love again, not realizing what I had was never love in the first place. I stayed in relationships through cheating, name-calling. fighting - you name it.

In 2011, the depression spirit took hold of me. I would literally cry myself to sleep every night. I wasn't happy, felt like I could not do anything right. I was always arguing at home and then, I was having issues at the job, being called into the office every week. During this time, I felt like I couldn't do anything right. My concentration was so off at work. I couldn't remember what someone had told me, because all throughout the day negative thoughts were racing through my head. At home, I was cursed out for any and almost everything. I felt worthless. I went to see a psychiatrist at my job. At first, they tried to diagnose me with ADD, but when the doctor did further testing, the diagnosis changed to depression and became medicated daily. Again, I also had high blood pressure, my stress levels were through the roof. I was broken and no matter how many compliments I got, about being this good parent, or the fact that I work and don't sit at home did not make a difference at all to the truth that I knew about myself, my mistakes and my own feelings. At this point I almost felt beyond repair.

Chapter Twelve
Why did we get Married?

After the altercation between Tyray and I at my friends Father's Day party, Tyray became very angry with me, because I placed him on child support through the judicial system. It took a while for him to be comfortable picking up Serenity. But after a few months, he began to come around. Dacia had a birthday party and I invited Tyray niece and nephew. Which means Tyray must bring them to the party. Whenever Tyray would come by the house my daughter Tiffany, would always ask can he stay, I would always say NO, but this time I said yes. It was a result of me giving in to the spirit of loneliness. We talked all night and eventually ended up getting back together. I told him, this time we would not work. At first, he thought I was joking, and he would try to leave whatever items he had at my house, but I would follow him to the door saying, "oh no, take this with you." We began couples counseling and decided that we would get married. (The problem with this, 2 years prior to this counseling session, Tyray and I saw a Christian counselor and she gave it to us plainly, straight, no chaser WE SHOULD NOT BE TOGETHER, neither of us took heed to that rebuke) His family was not happy about the union at all. One of his sisters, stopped talking to him for a while. We decided to go to City Hall to get married. I went to a church close to my house, and asked the Pastor there to bless our wedding rings. While he blessed the rings, he asked me, if I would like for him to marry us. I said, "I sure would love that." So, a few weeks later we were married in the Pastor's office. We continued counseling sessions only for a short while after this. We were on our way to a counseling session and Tyray looked at me and said, "I don't think we need this anymore, we are doing good and we know what we need to do." I didn't agree at first, but after listening to him, I thought that things would OK and maybe he was right. This time we seemed to be doing better than ever, but things began to change to having to move, because the apartment we lived in was in foreclosure.

We moved to Willowbrook, Illinois in 2012, to a three-bedroom apartment, but the arguments and fights began all over again. This time he was trying to blame me for cheating. One example that comes to mind is when my aunt Ingrid came to Chicago, she rented a hotel room for us and a few of her best friends. These were the same women that were around when I was younger. I had Tyray to drop me off at the hotel. Now, my aunt Ingrid came down to the car and spoke to Tyray, "So you would expect for the night of be great right since he knows where I am and who I am with?" Wrong. Tyray called me in the middle of the night, saying I was out with a man and he was tired of me, because I was out cheating on him. Really!! After you just dropped me off to my aunt, someone who raised me as her own child? All the ladies are hearing Tyray fuss and accuse me of cheating on him. They all looked at me, and said, "the only reason he is lashing out that way is because he is guilty of cheating on me." I didn't even allow him to pick me up the next day. One of my aunt's friends dropped me off at home.

When I get home, I was not much for words, I just wanted to relax. I go to the bedroom and he starts an argument, so I decide to take a breather and chill out in my oldest daughter's room, just to escape the madness. Later on, I am walking to the kitchen, but I hear him whispering on the phone, so I began to walk a little softer. When I reach the front room, Tyray is still whispering. I walk over to him and he looks at me with a surprised look on his face. I say to him, "This is the reason you are accusing me. Usually I would snap but this day I just walked away.

The following day, I had to take my car to the repair shop and I had to have Tyray pick me up. As we are in the car I began to pick his brain a little. I told him, "I know it's a girl he has been texting and speaking to." I began to tell him what their conversations were about. I thought I made all these accusations up in my mind, but everything I said I was right on target. I truly believe it was the Holy Spirit downloading this information into my spirit. All I kept saying to myself was, "God did you give me all this information?" Anyway, the look on his face was priceless, and all Tyray kept saying, was how did you know that? Who told you all of this? I told him if he tells me who it was, I would tell him how I got the information. After he told me who it was, which I perceived that to be a lie as well, I also lied and told him I went to the Cheaters Spy Store and purchased a device that retrieves deleted text messages. He believed it, and he began to call me a stalker. You get caught cheating on your wife, and you think you have any room or leverage to call me a stalker? Absolutely not.

A few months later an Evangelist got a calling from God to plant a church in the complex, for resident and surrounding areas. She asked if I would be her nurse for the church and if my kids would be praise dancers. This pastor began to counsel me and

Tyray. But once again, this helped in the beginning, but the fighting continued and then went to worse. Being with the Pastor my fight became different. I would run down to her house and let her pray for me and give me guidance. Things began to escalate, Tyray would come in from work arguing. I mean who comes home from work arguing about peanut butter, or about the patio blinds whatever. I have the house quiet and clean, food cooked, but you much come in and find something to argue about. When he would come in like this, I would go to my car. Most night I would sit in my car and cry out to God and ask him what did I do wrong? Or, why have I done so wrong to be treated this way? Then I began to take my bible out to the car with me and I would sit cry out and read until I believed Tyray was passed out sleep and then go back into the house.

After 9 months of living in the apartments we could move into the town homes. We were still on shaky ground. By this time my friend Charmaine and her now ex-husband would come over and hang out with us on the weekends. Everything was great at first until her husband started acting up as well. At this point me and Charmaine are saying to one another, "These two are over here twinning with attitudes." Things got so bad that me and Charmaine pulled a Tina move when her and Ike had that last fight. We went to the LaQuinta Hotel and told the front desk concierge, our husbands were acting irrational and we need a place to stay the night for us and our kids, so they blessed us with a room we didn't have to pay for. Our arguments became more frequent when his Job began to threaten a shut down. More Alcohol was involved. Everyone saw what how alcohol altered who he was, so much so that my oldest daughter would take his bottle of alcohol and pour it out. When that wasn't working, my kids resorted to another resolution. I would come home on Friday night from work and my kids would have their bags packed for us to go to the hotel, or to the kids Aunt Sherry's house, because they knew it was Friday and what would happen once Tyray started drinking. This is when I got tired and fed up.

    We got into an argument on a Sunday night, but I just went upstairs to my room. From the time we moved into the townhouse, Tyray pretty much slept in the basement, because we were always arguing. I got used to sleeping alone at this point, but Monday morning comes and it's time for me to go to work. I took Serenity downstairs to him. You could tell he was still very intoxicated from the night before. I tried to pass him Serenity but, he jumped up and began cursing me out and said, "If I leave her with him, he would call the police on me and say I left her at the house alone." So, I said, "Boy, whatever!" And tried to pass him the baby, but he pushed us into the recliner. I said I am not about to fight this morning, so I called the police and told them, I wanted him out. He began to act big shot and say things like, "Oh I'm happy to get out of here" and "Ain't no way I'm staying with a woman that would call the police on me for nothing." He began to talk about how he would come and pick up his stuff another day.

    He began to harass me and threaten me over the phone. So, the police officer that escorted him out, called him and told him, if he continues to call me and threaten me, they would take him into custody. Then, Tyray started a rumor that I was having an affair with the police officer because the officer called about the harassment on my behalf. No! The man was just doing his job. So, I went and filed for a divorce. My marriage only lasted a year and a half, but I was with him 7 years. Tyray agreed with the divorce at first. This divorce process went so fast, we were divorced in less than a month. I did all the paperwork myself, represented myself, Tyray agreed to the terms and the process was over with speedily. It wasn't until after the divorce Tyray began to flip out. I received the most disrespectful phone calls in the middle of the night from Tyray, although this was short-lived it was hurtful and annoying. This only confirmed that I made the right decision.

Although Tyray and I didn't make it, he is an amazing father to Serenity. Our co-parent relationship is great as well. Since this we have apologized to one another and have moved forward smoothly in our own lives. We must forgive so that we may release all that may hinder us spiritually.

I continued to attend the church and began to grow spiritually. I began to learn about speaking in tongues and this was my first time, hearing about or seeing deliverance. I became very interested and desires the gift speak in tongues so bad the Pastor would often pray over me to help me receive, but nothing would happen. I learned about the fruit of the Spirit and how to apply it to my life. I was taught to read my bible daily. Now honestly even though I was doing all this I was still in mega bondage. I still had a fear of being alone and I still fornicated. I called myself dating, one might say desperately. It started with me dating this guy in a wheelchair and come to find out he had more problems than that and I had no other choice but to let that go. I was close with one of my church members, her name was Kim. I became Godmother to her Grandson Jayden. We were with each other daily, this didn't help either of our walks with Christ, because we too were two broken people trying to counsel one another. We coached each other into staying in wrong relationships. If she liked the guy I was dating, she would call me evil and say I haven't even given the guy a chance and how she would feel sorry for the guy if I broke up with him and he was trying to get me back. So, I would take her advice and she would take mines. We were the blind leading the blind. I remember her youngest son called both of us desperate. Although he was maybe 10 years old at the time, his words may have been disrespectful, but it held a lot of truth.

Chapter Thirteen

Lord, I Wanna be Free!

2014, things really began to change for me. I grew an interest in deliverance and began to buy books to read and become more knowledgeable. I was so intrigued by it, I asked my Pastor at the time to mentor me in deliverance. I thought I could go to her because she introduced me to deliverance, plus she was like a mother to me. She gave me love and rebuke at the same time. It seemed her rebukes came from genuine place in the beginning. She refused to teach me more about deliverance and told me, not to read anything about demons unless it was on soul ties. She also told me, if you don't know what you are doing demons can kill you. This was one of the rebukes I didn't heed to. I began to buy all the John Eckhardt books I could find and any other books that would deal with the subject of deliverance. I would read and listen to sermons on deliverance and holiness daily. I still wasn't exhibiting much freedom at the time from fornication, but I was able to stop cursing and drinking alcohol. This cursing was hard for me to give up. It seemed the more I prayed to God about it, the worse my mouth became. My children tried a curse jar, but that only made them richer every day. With this stronghold, I learned the power of what I like to call, "Not in my own strength." Once I gave up and took my hands off the issue, God's grace kicked in and the cursing went away suddenly. And the taste for Alcohol just left as well. I was beginning to experience freedom, just at a slow pace.

The one spirit that I had to break free from was control and manipulation that has run down my bloodline. I have even seen it manifest in myself in romantic relationships as well as with my own children. In my family, I have seen this spirit cause guilt, fear, bitterness and shame to name a few. It can also cause the person operating in this spirit to be a compulsive liar. They can look you straight in the face and lie on you, and/or lie to you. This spirit manifest with crying to get one's way, or degrading a person to make them feel inferior, or what you think to be a reverse psychology method as well as financially control. For example, Your Teen or adult children are at home and you take their whole checks and make them feel as if you need them there to pay the bills, so if they desired to get out on their own, this spirit makes them feel guilty, which will cause the person not to venture out and experience life for themselves. How about a parent taking total care of the teen or adult making the child fear they won't be able to make it in the real world on their own? Also, what I like to call tit-for-tat, which means when someone says, they are not going to do anything for a person, who has told them no. This is a form of control to try to make the other person feel guilty about saying no. If you won't do this for me, then I won't do that for you, and they will hold it over the person's head. There is also a divide and conquer spirit, causing you to isolate yourselves from friends and family. These are just a few ways this spirit has operated from what I have seen in my family lineage.

    The spirit of manipulation and control is very real and most times we do not know we are operating in this spirit. We have picked up habits from the older generations, because it was a learned behavior and it was done to us. Now, when you become educated and understand what you are dealing with, you will change because you see how this can affect the people you love, relationships, even your own life. But there are some who know they are being deceitful and still carry own with this spirit as if it is healthy practice.

In relationships, I tried to make a man feel terrible for wanting to break up, by making them feel guilty. Also, yelling and fussing at a man about what he was or wasn't doing. This was a control tactic because it was often accompanied by a threat of me leaving the man if things didn't go my way. I saw even my daughter picking up this pattern. My oldest daughter saw me do this a lot with my ex-husband to try to gain control of whatever situation or argument we were in. I would always threaten to leave him, if he wouldn't do what I wanted him to do. I would not do things for him, because he would not do certain things for me and throw it in his face, so that he knows why and to inflict guilt upon him.

When it came to my children, I would use comparison between the children to try and manipulate them to do better. If my children did wrong, I would use silent treatment as a form of punishment. I remember how my Grandmother would give me the silent treatment if I didn't go to church on a Sunday when I hung out the night before. I did all this believing it was right, because it was what I learned until I was taught about how this spirit manifest and I became knowledgeable and desired to be set free.

In June 2014, my oldest daughter graduated from High School, and my mother fell on hard times and lost her home. I couldn't see my mom without a place, so I told her to come live with me until she got on her feet. My daughter was going away to college so she didn't mind giving up her basement for her grandmother. As my Mom moved in, everything started out just fine, but began to take a turn for the worst. We had a family outing to Six Flags Great America, it started out great until we were about to go home. Dacia and Keke were in an argument, and my mother was with them. My mother approached me and began to go off about how, she will not be disrespected by anybody, not even her grandchildren. As I got more detail from her, she told me how Keke mistreated her and she didn't do anything but try to talk to her, she said she didn't put her hands on her or anything to make her feel uneasy. So, when Keke finally walked up, I instantly grabbed my child around her collar about to put her in her place about disrespecting my mother. My daughter started crying and saying, "Momma, what I do? She hit me, all I did was walk away so me and Dacia would stop arguing!" Then my cousin Cece grabbed me and said, "Keke didn't do anything Nikki!" So, I asked them what happened, their story was different from my mother's interpretation. So, I asked a few others that was around and they told me the same thing Keke and Cece told me. Now at this point I am hurt, and had to apologize to my child and then, I confronted my Mom and asked her, why she wasn't honest about hitting Keke. I believe in discipline so if it was something she did, all she had to do was tell me that she disciplined her grandchild. This caused a breach in our relationship and I became cautious and defensive with my mother regarding my kids.

The next incident happened when invited a guy over to

meet her who I had been dating for a little while, but I knew him from 7th and 8th grade. She had never met him, but in grammar school he was one of the people that I told I was molested. I told him because I was close with him in grammar school at the time my mother's boyfriend molested me. When he reached out to me on Facebook, he had to tell me exactly who he was for 2 reasons. I had buried the memories of those years, plus he looked different, his head had caught up with his body and he was handsome. After him becoming reacquainted I asked him to come in the house to meet my Mother. When he arrived, my mom ran down to the basement. While waiting on her to come back upstairs, I got a text and from my mom. The text read, "You shouldn't have bought him here, it's too soon!" I texted her back, I invited him here to meet you, and what type of statement is that to make, when you have no idea how long I had even been seeing this guy." Needless to say, she didn't come back upstairs.

A few weeks later we decided to go to church together. My male friend as well as my kids is in the kitchen while I am upstairs in my room still getting ready for church. The kids later ask me once I am dressed and moving around the house, "Did you hear what Grandma said to your friend, she wasn't really nice at all." By this time my male friend had gone out to the car to wait for me. I told the kids that I hadn't heard and before I could ask the kids what happened, I heard my Mom coming up from the basement, so I told my children to just wait and tell me later. I told them to head outside, because they would usually take a ride with my mother to the church. As the kids were on their way out the door, my mom has this disgusted look on her face and she walks up to me, and begin to tell me how she didn't like the company being here, and right in the mist of her telling me what she did not like, I had to stop her and put her in her place and let her know that is not her call. My mother stormed out angry and headed to the church.

I get in the car to ask what happened and my male friend begin to explain that he spoke to my Mom and she didn't respond, so when she walked past again he said, "Good Morning" for the second time, because he said he thought she did not hear him the first time. My mother responded back, "I don't speak to men this early in the morning. And he said he responded, "Oh I'm sorry to hear that." Now I asked my children when I arrived at the church, because church had not started and they told me the exact same thing. So, at this point, I'm like all right no big deal, it's over with. But that was far from the truth

After service was over, we had a church meeting. I saw my mother walk over to my friend and she began to talk to him. Now I am more focused on my mother and male friend, because I know this isn't going to turn out good. And sure, enough it did not. I see the conversation is escalating between the 2 of them, so I excuse myself from the meeting and as I am walking over to them, my mom begins to walk away quickly. A few members heard the whole conversation between them. My mother walked over to tell him, she was sorry for not speaking back to him that morning, but he shouldn't have been there because he is not any of my children father's. My male friend said, he apologizes and he asked her whose house was it, hers or mine? My mom responded it's the Lords house! Now I am upset. I told my mom if she does not want to respect my house she does not have to be there and she can to leave. She was very upset about my response and decided to call the pastor over to speak with me about the gentleman. There was one mistake doing this, I had already informed my Pastor that my male friend would be accompanying me to church and I already sat with her and told her a lot about my male friend. My mom wasn't expecting any of that. She denied everything she said to my male friend at the church. This was the same dishonesty I spoke with her about at the amusement park. Denial of her actions and not taking responsibility for it. My mother began to talk about how I wasn't raised right by my grandmother and how it was almost as if my grandmother tried to pimp me. My mother gave an example, because I needed clarity on this. This was new to me, so she began to speak about how my Grandmother brought me some shorts and my uncle's employees (he owned a construction company) were eyeballing and drooling over me. She told the pastor that I was being abused. I said, "No, I was not." My Mom responded, "Yes you were, you were too young to understand what was going on." Then she went on to say my grandmother's boyfriend was physically abusing me. I stopped her and reminded her that, he was sexually abusing me, and not beating me. At that point, she tried to say she didn't know that happened. I believed she said she didn't know that happened because she didn't expect for that information to come out in front of the pastor. I had to again remind her that she did know that it was sexual because I remember as a little girl, when my mother came home on leave and was very angry about him touching me sexually and slept with the gun under her pillow. I also reminded her about when it was her boyfriend who molested me and she told me, "Whatever happens in this house stays in this house." Thankfully the Pastor calmed us both down and resolved this issue.

That very phrase, "What happens in this house stays in this house" is what has kept my family in bondage. I know my mom got this phrase from her mother because I have heard my grandmother say this about other things. My grandmother would tell me that, so I don't go telling people when my Aunt and Uncle got into fights or private conversations. But nonetheless it was a common phrase upheld in our home; darkness that the enemy cultivated and dwelt in: *Isolation*.

This spirit also can cause the victim to be isolated or go into isolation. This spirit can even cause the person operating in this spirit to go into isolation as well. Let me give you an example how this tried to come for me. When my mom moved with me I only had two female friends that I would spend time with. The first incident was the church back to school event. One of my friends were on snowball duty and the snowballs came in 50 cents or a dollar size cups. My mom decided to purchase a 50-cent snowball and all my friend had left at her booth were the dollar cups, so she half-way filled the cup with ice and snowball juice. Then the Pastors teenage, son walks over and buys a dollar snowball. My friend fills his cup with ice and juice. This made my mother angry and she began to rant and rave at my friend about it. Rather than, my friend being her true self and giving my mother a piece of her mind, she respected her because she was my mother. My friend just walked off and reported to the Pastor the incident. The Pastor came out and said to all of us, "I WANT ALL OF YOU TO WORK YOUR OWN BOOTH. DON'T WORRY ABOUT

ANYBODY ELSE'S, THIS IS FOR THE CHILDREN WHO ARE GOING BACK TO SCHOOL!" After that, my Mom walks over to me, saying how my friend is sneaky and she doesn't want her over to the house anymore. I plainly told my mother, "She can and will be allowed at my house." My Mom was upset and said, "You are going to choose her over me?" I told my mother it is not about that, right is right and wrong is wrong, no matter who it is.

    The second incident was with my friend Keisha who has been in my life for 20 years. Keisha knows my grandmother and aunt Ingrid, but she was just introduced to my mother a few months prior to this incident. My mother obviously didn't know the extent of our friendship. This is when strange things began to happen. Keisha and I took my oldest daughter to college at SIUC to help her set up her dorm and we came back the very next day. I left my spare key at home. Keisha was attending church with me at the time, so our weekends were spent at my house. After leaving SIUC and coming back to Chicago, I dropped Keisha off at home and she decided, once she got her kids together she would head to my house for the weekend. I get home and decide to take a quick nap before my friend and her tribe arrives. We left a few items in my car, so when Keisha called my cell phone and told me, she was about to pull up, I told her I would unlock the door so that our kids could remove the items from the car and bring them in the house. I always kept the spare key on my dresser, since that was the first key I saw, I hit the unlock button on the key fob, but to my surprise it was not working. No big deal, right? Maybe there's something wrong with it, I have another key. I go downstairs and grab the other key fob, now that one is not working. Let me remind you, I just got finished utilizing this key. I just locked the car door a couple hours earlier and it was only my kids and my mother at the house.

It was too late to go to the dealer that day, so I decided to go to the dealership the next day. Me and my friend Keisha got up and rode to Kingdom Chevy to ask them what was wrong with my Key Fobs. They called us to the back… Now don't you laugh at us, like the people from the dealership did. They opened the key fobs and showed us that there were no batteries in either key fob. I said, "Are you sure it was batteries in there, because nobody opened it up to take them out, plus it worked yesterday for me, just fine until I got home." They laughed at me and Keisha because we were both standing there with the dumbest look. They give me two brand new batteries and put one in each Key Fob. Now they are both working appropriately. Still puzzled, but I leave the keys in the dining room overnight. I get up the very next morning and I grab the keys to go to church, and I can't unlock the doors with the Key Fob again. Now one is working, but the other is not. I open the Key Fob that is not working and guess what? The battery is missing again.

So, I am freaking out asking all the kids if they touched my keys, asking my mom as well. Then Keisha and I went to each kid asking him or her to open the key to see if any of them knew what they were doing. Not one of our kids knew how to open the key fob. I couldn't concentrate all while I was in church service. Me and Keisha just kept making eye contact like what could have possibly happened. Now that morning I planned to make fish for dinner, so I had it in a bowl of cool water to thaw out, so that it would be ready to cook once we all got out of church. You know church folk are ready to eat when they get out of service. As I began to drain the water off the fish, guess what I was in the fish water? Yep, the battery that was missing from my key. I am so happy that the whole family and my friend Keisha and her kids were in the kitchen to witness the battery in the fish water. My mom snatches the battery out of my hand quickly dries it off and tell me to check and see if it works, and if it doesn't she has an extra one this size. I didn't need my mom's battery that battery worked just fine. But Keisha and me could not help but talk about this until it was late and she had to go home. I mean my sleep that night was awful, because I was completely baffled about this key issue.

The following weekend Keisha and her children came over again, as usual, and guess what? My battery came up missing again. This time I went around the house asking the kids. I won't lie I began to suspect my mother, because stuff like this wasn't happening before now. So, I told Tiffany to go tell my mom to let me see the battery just to check if it fits. I told them, don't tell her the battery is missing. The kids came back up and told me that my Mom said, "Y'all don't even have to tell me the battery is missing again." I didn't suspect Keisha, because if that was something she wanted to try, she could have tried this long before because we had plenty of ladies' nights at my house and nothing ever came up missing. Plus, when you were around someone almost 20 years you pretty much know what they would try to pull. After this third time, I remember taking a shower and pouring out my heart to God about this and asking him to not allow me to lose my mind.

The Spirit of control and manipulation also works to

demean. It is usually done and most effective by the authoritarian. It can happen between parent and child, knowingly or unknowingly. If it is multiple children in a home, you may even hear one child stating, "I am the black sheep of the family." Usually a person feels this way because they felt or believed they couldn't live up to the standards of their other siblings. The Parent may say something like, "Why can't you be more like Johnny!" I have found myself doing this a lot between my children. Knowing that they are all different and develop different we must be careful not to compare our children to one another, especially to gain control believing you are sparking a flame to push them to do better. This spirit also manifest with negative statements like, "There's something wrong with you!" or "You think you are so smart! You ain't nobody special!" These are phrases I have heard done to the older generations in my family and it was passed down.

    Examples of how it was done to me; in 2015, my daughter decided to leave college and work full-time. By this time, I learned what the spirit of Jezebel (Control and Manipulation) in the family looked like even when it comes to adult children. As much as I wanted my daughter to remain in school, receive all the help see needed from me, that child was now 18 years old and I can't control what she wants to do at this point. She is no longer under my roof, so I can't tell her, "This is what it is, and this is how it is going to be." The hardest thing I had to learn to do, was cut the umbilical cord. Sometimes you should step aside and allow God to do the work, because all the parental bickering can sometimes do is push them further away. Had this been 2013 or 2014, I probably would have tried to control my adult child decision or even manipulated her into what I felt was best for her.

My Mother approached me about Keke leaving college and relocating to St. Louis. I told my mother all I could do was stay on the wall for her, that I can't make that decision for her, I will not continue to pay for something and force her to be somewhere she is not happy. My mother looked at me and said, "You have to do something, I don't want her to turn out like YOU." When she said that I walked away, cause I needed to process that. I went to my room and thought to myself, "OK my mom didn't mean that, she couldn't have, it had to be just a bad choice of words, I'm going to just let it go.

A few weeks later, my mother approaches me again regarding Keke leaving college. She'd been talking to Keke and trying to get her to change her mind about school. My mom says, "Nikki she is making a big mistake leaving school, have you even tried talking to her." I told her again, "I won't tell an adult child, that wants to be independent what to do, and nor will I force her to stay somewhere she is not happy." My mother looked at me and said, "I just don't want her to turn out like you." I said to myself, "okay she means this statement, this is the second time she said this. She wants me to hear it loud and clear." Now I am livid. I asked my mom, "WHAT DO YOU MEAN TURNED OUT LIKE ME?" My mother looked at me and said, "Look at you, you're still in school." Honestly all I could think about was an incident that happened when I was younger. My Aunt Ingrid and I were filling out FAFSA papers when I graduated from High School. My mother looked at us and said I don't know why you are filling out those papers, it's not like she is going to go to College. My Aunt

Ingrid told me not to look up, just keep filing out the paperwork. I felt no matter what I did as far as furthering my education it was degraded by my mother. That was College but this time I was taking bible classes at Living Word Christian Center for ministry. My mother proceeded and said, "that is a generational curse, look at Ingrid. She is almost 50 in school to be a nurse and you are still in school." I said, "so, if a person decides to go back to school, it's considered a curse? Out of all the deliverance books I have been reading, I have never heard of the continuing education demon." Now I tried to snap in the most respectful way I could, but I don't believe I was successful. She tried to tell me that I took that the wrong way, and I was taking it too far. I don't know how this can be misinterpreted.

Those words in the spirit were set to belittle me and to make me feel inferior, and I had to remember who I am and whose I am.

"The spirit of manipulation is skilled in tying adult children to parental cords for a long time so they can't live their lives or be independent. It uses guilt as a trap to benefit the user buy destroys the recipient" -*Belinda Enoma*

Chapter Fourteen

No Devil, You Won't Trick Me This Time!

In 2014, my relationship with the pastor began to change, and not for the better. I would be called out during church service almost every Sunday, even when I made the decision to remain pure until marriage. I would talk to my pastor about everything, regarding relationships, my children, my job you name it. After feeling humiliated in front of the church on Sundays, I began to seek God harder on my own. I never went to my pastor for gossip or just to tell her how my day went, but I confided in her. The things I would tell her about were the issues I needed help and mentoring in. I wanted answers! See, now I didn't know that I could hear God on my own, so I would seek my pastor to get a word. I believe the humiliation I was enduring was God dealing with me for looking to MAN for answers. During my seek, God began to show me the root cause of the lust spirit that I was bound to.

The Holy Spirit began to work with me and show me the steps that I needed to take. I came from a family that did not know the power of soul ties, the meaning or true understanding of sex. Sex was not dealt with on a spiritual level, but more so based upon age. I was always told, you're too young to have sex. What they were taught, is that it was normal to have sexual feelings and thoughts of sex even as a young child. This way of thinking was passed down to us. My family would tell me things like, when you are ready for sex, come and let us know so that we can start you on birth control, and I was only 12 or 13 years old. I even put my oldest daughter on birth control at a very young age because I felt she was on the verge of becoming sexually active. The summer of 2014, with the prompting of the Holy Spirit, because I was being taught about the spirits that held me captive and I desired to be set free, I began to attack this spirit. I was set free from pornography and masturbation first. In my closet, I had a lock box with all types of little sexual trinkets. I grabbed that along with all the DVD's and took it to the dumpster. After breaking up with the guy I was dating, I decided to try to keep myself for the first time.

In December 2014 I was doing good practicing abstinence for a while until the enemy sent another guy my way. This was a guy I called myself dating in grammar school. That little kiddie play that just shouldn't be allowed, you're my boyfriend. Had no idea what we were even talking about at that age. Anyway, we reconnected as adults and began to see one another on a regular. One day he decided to visit my church, and he joined. The Pastor called me later that evening and said, "Nikki you remember I said, someone is going to come into your life, and he is going to love you, but your love for him will have to grow?" I said, "Yes." She then said, "That's him!" I took her word for it. After two months, he decided he wanted to get married. He proposed to me on Valentine's Day 2015 at the Pastors house. Even at this point I am not gaining much feeling, yet allowing the Pastors words to flow though my head I kept trying to see if I would gain much attraction to him.

Then one day we are over a friend's house and it gets too late to go home. We end up staying the night and one thing led to another, and ultimately ended in us having sex. This is when I found out had to learn boundaries in dating. Why didn't I learn about this before!! We all have certain triggers and being pure until marriage, we must know what they are and how to stay away from them. The next day was Sunday and my God sister was scheduled to preach at my old church where I grew up, so we decided to go there to support her for Sunday service. On the way to the church I kept telling him, how I have messed up my purity and I need to repent. And he responded, "It's OK, if you want to stop, we don't have to do that anymore until we are officially married." We get to the church and my sister's whole sermon is about how God is willing to give you another chance to get it right. That message was convicting me something awful.

After being sexually active with this man, I began to see his jealous side. We were at my friend's baby shower and I was taking pictures for her. It was another guy there, who was toned and you knew that he worked out. We just so happened to be standing next to one another. No words were exchanged or anything, nor did we look in one another's direction. Once we leave the baby shower, while in the car, he looked at me and said, "I was a little jealous that guy with all those muscles standing next to you, I didn't like that." I didn't allow him to see my reaction, because I didn't know how that would make him react. I began to become cautious and calculate my steps with this guy. Arguments began to increase. He would get upset because I was on my cell phone either on Facebook or texting a friend. He was upset because I would refuse to have sex with him, he would listen in on all my phone conversations. Should I say, things began to get real. I Google searched him, and I found that this man has a "Domestic battery/ Bodily Harm" on his record. So, I ask him had he ever hit a woman. He told me some story that landed him in jail with a domestic. This guy was controlling already and we are not married at all yet. Oh, let me not forget, this is the only guy my mother and the Pastor really seemed to like a lot and they approved of him.

Let me tell you how I fixed the problem. I told him I was going on a fast, while I am on this fast a lot of things are happening and it's happening quickly. We were allowing the kids to gain a relationship, so him and kids came over and I allowed them to all stay downstairs on the first floor of my townhouse. I also allowed one of my friend's daughters over that weekend and all the children decided to prank call people they knew. The kids decided to prank call my friend, but it got a little out of hand and my fiancée son got disrespectful and cursed at my friend's husband. My friend called me and let me know what happened and I apologized. My fiancée at the time didn't really address this issue. When my friend and her husband came to pick up their child the next day, we sat down to discuss the matter, but my so-called fiancée walked off and left me in the conversation all alone (How about that). I again, apologized on the child's behalf. When they left, I went and found him, I asked him why did he walk away, and he said, "Because he didn't want to hear that." My reaction to this was, "Let me get this straight, you want to be in MY conversation if I am talking on the phone, but if it is regarding your child, you care not to listen in, nor have an opinion or apology on that?" This is not the type of man I see myself with for the rest of my life.

It gets a little better, so him and his best friend are not

working together now, but he finds a job and needs to use my car. Now I have OnStar and the ability to track my car where ever. This day, he had court regarding one of his kids that DCFS had taken from the mother. Allow me to remind you, I am still fasting. I begin to pray, "OK God if this is not the guy for me, give me one more sign." Sure enough, I got answered swiftly.

Never had I checked OnStar to locate my car, but the Holy Spirit spoke to me. I called him and asked him what was he doing, and where was? Well, he wasn't honest with me about his whereabouts. My car was parked in front of his child's mother home, the same one who he was in court with. I didn't say anything right then, because I knew he had a meeting with the Pastor later that evening. I quickly informed the pastor that day that I was calling off the engagement and the reason why. Once him and the Pastor's meeting was over, I dropped him off at home, when I pulled off I called him while I was on my way home and told him, it was over, all the reasons why I no longer want to pursue a relationship with him and good-bye. He tried for a little while to get back, but shortly gave up. I also gave him back his engagement ring.

Let's talk more about this spirit of control and manipulation, which is also known as Jezebel or witchcraft. I have experienced this spirit in 3 ways at one time. The enemy surely had a contract on my life, my destiny and my purpose. I know I didn't touch too much on the church. In the church, it was my public humiliation, then control of who I was to fellowship with. Some members had left the church and decided to fellowship at another church. These were people I were close to, I remember getting an email from a minister at the church, stating how they are just looking out for my soul and to cut all ties with those members that left the church. Neither did I heed to these instructions, in fact I challenged it. I explained what the name of that church meant, and no matter what, when we see them because we are Christians we should show nothing but love, not bitterness, anger nor rejection. I asked, why would I want to be a part of a body that is taught to demonize people because they decide to change membership for their own personal growth or personal reason.

  This man I was engaged to have a demonic control spirit. In romantic relationships we must be careful, of the words we speak as well. This guy would tell me after we were engaged that, I already belonged to him, I would quickly break those words to his face, "No I don't, I belong to God." Every tongue that rises against you, YOU shall condemn. Our words have power and carry much weight in the spirit. You can be manipulated into staying connected with an ungodly soul tie. You ever heard someone say, "If you leave me, I will kill myself" OR "If you leave me I will kill you." This too is a form of witchcraft. This can cause guilt, as well as fear so the person remains trapped. Physical and verbal abuse are forms of control/witchcraft spirits. The main goal for this spirit is to impart fear and guilt.

  The flip side to this, children can also carry this spirit with the parent. When they cry because they do not get their way is a form of manipulation and if we don't get a hold of it in our babies it turns to full-blown witchcraft.

  In the workplace, this spirit can also manifest. Authority abusers are what they are called. They throw their title around as a form to say, you have to jump when I say jump, or else. I use titles as an example, because it doesn't have to be the boss, supervisor, or CEO. It may just be someone, who has been there longer than you or the rank of his or her title is higher than yours.

Getting set free from this spirit takes some warring, but you can do it. Whether it is you operating in this spirit (Jezebel) or you are being controlled and dominated by it (Ahab). Even if you fear this spirit from the outside and it is just after your gift and anointing (Elijah) you can defeat and obliterate this spirit from your life.

Chapter Fifteen

Prepare for Battle!

After the engagement was called off I rededicated myself to purity and this time I began to do more studying and read more books about maintaining my purity until marriage and learning boundaries. Now I was prepared, this was it, my body had been through enough. I had a chance to be born again, and do things the way God intended. But this spirit doesn't give up without a fight. It all starts with a bold decision!! In the beginning, I really had to affirm myself daily, I had post it notes with scripture all around the house, to go along with the daily affirmations. I Found out the strongman attached to the lust spirit was rejection. We can go through deliverance, which starts the road to freedom, but YOU maintain your deliverance in battle. Learning my Identity in Christ is the Key. Same for you.

Some battles had many long nights of spiritual warfare. God speaks to me mostly through dreams. Ever been awakened out of your sleep in fear, hearing someone call your name, but no one is there? We know God can at times speak to us in an audible voice. Although this is a rare occurrence, this experience is not accompanied with a spirit of fear. When you are awakened by a voice that causes fear there is a demonic presence around.

Warfare training for me began at home. When I was younger and I stayed in our family home, I would always be awakened in fear. When I moved from that house, it no longer happened to me. I didn't know about demonic spirits growing up, although I was raised in the church, it wasn't a subject that was ever touched in my old church. I was unaware that being awaken in fear was even demonic. In 2015 this started happening again, and then it happened to one of my daughters.

While sleeping one night, I was awakened by a familiar voice and it was accompanied by fear. My mother was living with me at the time. Because it sounded like my mother, I literally jumped up. My heart was pounding. I ran to the stairs and said, "What's wrong?" It was one of those, angry yells. When I made it to the stairs, no one was there. I went downstairs to look around, but again no one was there. I went back to my bed, but I knew then I had to do some praying.

When it happened to my daughter Tiffany, it was a few months later. I heard her yell out, and run toward the stairs. I asked her what was wrong and she told me, she heard someone call her name. I told her it was OK, and she could go back to bed, because no one called her. The Holy Spirit told me to ask her who it sounded like. When I asked her, she said, "It sounded like Grandma and I thought I was in trouble." This is the same thing I heard. The next day, my children and I began prayer together. This is when I began to teach my kids how to pray. At the time, my children and me would attend Living Word services and I had taken the intercessory prayer training class there. One of the advantages of going to a word of faith church, they teach you how to pray the Word. I put together some scriptural warfare prayers and wrote them out for my children to pray daily.

My daughter Dacia, also had a different type of experience with a demonic presence. After walking her youngest sibling to school, she said during her walk back to the house, she felt someone following her, but as she kept looking behind her, no one was there. Dacia said this presence followed her into the house. Dacia said she went to the bathroom on the second floor of our townhouse. We had a puppy named Teddy Bear. Teddy Bear began barking at the top of the stairs, and Dacia looked downstairs, but nothing was there. My daughter cried out Jesus twice and Teddy Bear stopped barking and walked down the stairs to the first floor. Therefore, it's so important to teach and include your children in prayer. It is never too early to teach a child demonology and warfare. Had I not been proactive in teaching my children what I was learning, she would have never known what to do in a spiritual attack and she would have been ignorant to the evil presence and would not have understood what was going on.

More demonic activity occurred at my house that my children, my best friend Keisha, and her children witnessed in October 2015. I came home from work, it was a Friday night and Dacia looked at me and said, "Ma, we have to pray, Teddy Bear has been barking at that corner all day." Before I could say anything, my mother said, "Girl prayer isn't needed, this house is covered in the blood." I looked at Dacia and told her we will pray, and I went upstairs to my room to get comfortable for the evening. When I came back downstairs, the children ran to me and told me that Teddy Bear had been barking again and everybody witnessed. Then they explained the whole scenario to me. Dacia, once again, tells them, "It's something in that corner, for Bear to be barking and growling, it has to be evil." My mom told Dacia it was her angel. Dacia said, just like this, "That ain't no angel." My mom got a little aggressive and said, "That is my angel, Not anything EVIL!" They all got quiet and didn't debate. All the children including my best friend witnessed this.

The next day I blessed my home, but it seemed like it was met with much resistance. Me and the children began to get more aggressive in prayer. We went to praying and blessing the house 3 times a day, we started to throw secular CD's and DVD's away, anything with demonic symbols were also tossed. My children even got word that Hello Kitty was demonic in nature. Since the kids' bathroom had the Hello Kitty theme, Tiffany came home from school and asked could she throw it all away.

In October and November I was listening Dr. Matthew Stevenson, Apostle John Eckhardt and Prophet Brian Carn - heavy. Mysteriously, November 1st of 2015, I get an email through my Google account from someone portraying to be Brian Carn. The email, began talking about my purpose and then, it went to say how the enemy wanted to take me out by accident, which this had at that time implanted the spirit of fear. The next day the witch emailed me back, saying, "Obey and send money to a charity for my protection." I declined and told him I will not obey. The next day I was in a car accident on I55 expressway. I was riding in the middle lane during rush hour, I heard the car on the right side of me attempt to hit breaks, but he swerved left and hit me, and then pushed me into another car on my left side. The car that caused the accident got away. Now, how did this car get away so fast in traffic? I believe the reason I came out of that accident, without any bodily harm because I was praying in tongues when the accident happened. The weapon formed, but it didn't prosper.

My mother had to come pick me up because my car wasn't in driving condition at all. I became fearful to drive, so I needed some prayer warriors to help me push past this. I hadn't told anyone but a pastor what happened with the email. First, I called a Pastor to pray for me, but it was a Wednesday, so the Pastor couldn't come because the church had bible class. I also called two of my spiritual sisters. The first one came to pray with me and I asked if it was all right if we went out to the car. She began to speak with me about how she felt a strong demonic presence in my house that wants to take control, and it was coming from the basement (OK. My mom stayed in the basement, not what I wanted to hear, I was trying to get over a fear of driving and I have to face this? These, were my thoughts), how I need to continue to fight and begin to clean my house of all spirits. Then my other spiritual sister called because she couldn't make it over to the house, so she prayed for me while she was at work. She told me, that the spirit that was in my house was trying to cause me to lose my mind (When she said this all I could think about was the day I was in the shower crying out to the Lord when the Key batteries were coming up missing) and how I needed to put my big girl drawers on and have my mom get her own place. So now I am like, these are two different people telling me this. But now I am fearful, because it seems dishonorable to put your mother out, but God was calling me to do this. So now I get this bubbling feeling inside saying, "Who are you going to obey?" I quickly said, "Jesus!!!"

I knew my mother would not understand the angle I would come from with this. How do you tell your Mom that she has to leave without her feeling as if you don't love or care for her well-being? I made up a huge lie due to fear. I told her that management found out she was there and she had to go, when truthfully, I told management she was there and if I needed a note to evict her, what would the procedure consist of. Although I had prepared in case she refused to leave, I did not need to include them. She left with no problem the next day. The same day my mom leaves to go to a shelter, the pastor I originally called to pray for me, had another word for me regarding my mother. This Pastor too told me about a control and manipulation spirit that was on my mother. I then told that pastor, that I just had my mother to move out. The pastor told me that was good and to continue to intercede and pray nothing but blessings over my mother.

That same day I went down to the basement to gather my mother's belongings. I made up in my mind that I would put her stuff in storage and pay for 2 months myself, because my mother had so many souvenirs and keepsakes from around the world, I didn't know what gave legal ground for that demonic presence to be in my home. While putting her things together I found her Eastern Star shirt on the floor under her air mattress. At this moment I believe, that was confirmation from God that I had to put her stuff in storage and remove it from my home. As far as I knew she no longer had any connections to this secret keeping organization. At this time, she had been living in my house for a year, so for it to show up under her air mattress she had to have known that it was there. Learning about deliverance, spirits gain legal ground to your home by items that are in your home. Deuteronomy 7:26 reads, *neither shalt thou bring an abomination into thine house, lest thou be a cursed thing like it. But thou shalt utterly detest it, and thou shalt utterly abhor it, for it is something banned.* I packed all her items myself, although I had two males assist me with removing the items and place them is storage for me. My mom was so angry about me putting her stuff in storage that she made up a lie to make me feel guilty. The lie was, I threw her crystal ornaments away, which this wasn't the truth at all. I put the wall stands and the crystals in the same box and sealed them myself. My mother told me she had the wall stands, but her crystal ornaments were not in that box. Now there were few items I did throw away, I paid her for these items before she said her crystal ornaments were missing. The items I had to replace, or pay for were, her portable wardrobe closet that was already broken, and some dolly straps. But no way was I am falling for the crystal missing. As the two young men, were moving my mother's items out, my youngest daughter, Serenity, in whom my mom had the closet relationship, told us something and made us all stop what we were doing. My mother had a wooden rod and Serenity asked us, "What are ya'll doing with her grandmother's stick? It's magic and she told me it has powers." Serenity sealed the deal for me. That was total confirmation about the action I was taking. See, a lot of the time we don't know the artifacts and objects we may have in our home can carry evil spirits and it causes demonic activity. But even so, this is truly not something we want to hear about a parent, nor should make the decision to have your parent leave. Yet all these confirmations within a 24-hour period caused me to act. I had no other choice. Although we love her, I am not willing to allow my kids to be with her because of Serenity's statement.

As a parent, I must protect my children at all cost. I know there has been control and manipulation spirits that have run down our bloodline. Especially between parents and children. After my mother left, she began to miss her grandchildren and decided to pop up while I was at work. She told my daughters to give me her number. So, I called my mother and explained to her the reason why my children can't go to her house. I told her about the statement Serenity made regarding her wooden rod and the Eastern star shirt I found. I also told her another reason she wasn't allowed spend time with my kids was due to the breach in our relationship. She began to say how she never came between the relationship I had with my grandmother, but what she did not realize is that our relationship was a lot different from the one she had with my kids. My grandmother raised me when she left and went to the army. My mom made a statement about me saying that she abandoned me (Although I didn't make this statement, what I said was, if she is beating herself up for leaving me when I was 5 years old, to let it go, because I felt she did what she felt she had to do). During this conversation, I asked her, why did she leave me and decide the army was the best choice. She told me, she had no other choice, she was in school and my grandparents knew that she needed whatever cash she had for school, but they forced her to give up all her money and she couldn't finish school. (Making your children give you ALL their finances is another sign of control and manipulation in the home). She explained that her mother was unfairly treating her. I asked her if she felt her mother was mistreating her, why would she leave me there? My mother answered, "Because I know she wouldn't mistreat YOU, I saw the love she gave you still to this day she hasn't mistreated you." When my mother said this, I saw a contradiction in this statement. If you recall a few chapters back, when my mother called the Pastor over, my mother told my pastor I was being mistreated by my grandmother and that she wasn't raising me up, the way a young woman should be. I didn't ask my mother anymore questions regarding this, because I felt I would never get the truth out of my mother. We went back to why I put her items in storage. She tried to say that I hated her, which this is never the case. I told her because the bible tells us not to have any detestable things in our home. My mother asked me, where did I read that at in the bible. I told her about Deuteronomy 7:26, and I also screenshot the scripture and sent it to her phone so that she could see for herself. My mother then told me, "I never have nor will I ever take a biblical lesson from you!" I responded, "That's fine, but you asked so I sent you proof so that you may read it with your own eyes.

    My mother felt as if I didn't love her, which is far from the truth. I love my mom, but I must be obedient to what God is telling me to do. I know I shouldn't have lied regarding management finding out, but when you are not delivered and full of fear, this is what happens. This is why it is important to seek God in all situations. I didn't seek God when I asked my mother to move in, so I felt He would say, "You got yourself in this mess, now get yourself out." That was the orphan spirit running rampant in me. Had I sought God, I know he would have given me a plan to do this task with integrity and love. Honestly, we never know who or what we have to walk away from to get healing, BUT it is always better to do it with love boldly and in honesty, no matter who gets mad or doesn't understand. You have done your part as a child of God in obedience and integrity. I had to repent and break fear, because I honestly knew he wasn't through removing the people I had around me, and I needed boldness to explain to people the reason for the separation. I know sometimes you don't have to explain, but when you want to do things in love, I think its best in my opinion to give explanation. At least even if they don't understand you have still done your part. When God tells you to part from people, friends, family, lovers, you must move because this is about your growth and purpose in the Kingdom. God began to comfort and encourage me about having to walk away from someone who the bible tells you to honor, because although I did it, and it felt like the right thing to do, I would rather make sure I heard God on something this thick.

God began to speak though these scriptures, Luke 14:25-34 and Matthew 12:46-50. It wasn't that He didn't love his family, but they weren't in the will of the Father at that point, because they pretty much said Jesus was tripping and they set out for the temple to make him stop. Jesus was like, look I am about my Father's business right now, and not even you all can stop me. This is how God wants us all to be for him. It is not that you don't love people, but sometimes they are unaware that they are operating in these spirits and even if when you tell them, sometimes they will deny and even call you crazy. Even if they don't receive, you can separate yourself, but continue to intercede for them in love and remain peaceful. You have to separate yourself for your healing and deliverance maintenance, your Kingdom purpose, and so much more is based upon your obedience and who you have in your circle. Just as heaven has assigned mentors and connections, so does hell. Wrong people create stumbling blocks, but the right people help you build a wall with those blocks. Just like Nehemiah, we are born leaders and the people we have around us need to be effective and purposeful.

When in battle, it is very important that you know how to pray, your stance in prayer and well as the dominion you have in the Earth. Being at a faith based church, you are taught to pray the word of God. This is done by learning scriptures and writing them of the tablets of your heart (memorization). When Jesus was tempted in the wilderness, his armor was the word of God. He always responded with, "It is written…" Being taught to pray from a position of heaven to Earth also will make a powerful impact on your prayer life.

Learning spiritual warfare properly cause me to see victory in the areas of my mind, my home, on the job as well as removing fear that was planted by that witch/warlock on the internet before the car accident. It's equally important that you increase in faith just as much as it's important to learn scripture. These two work in partnership with one another because without faith, it's impossible to please God and faith comes by hearing the word of God.

This was also a time when God spoke to me about guarding my gates. Your spiritual gates are your eyes and ears. Aside from me throwing secular CD's and DVD's away, I was also mandated not to watch or listen to music that was lustful or demonic in nature. I was a huge Scandal and Empire fan. Although I had church on Wednesday I made sure to DVR Empire and watch it as soon as I returned home. My favorite music R&B by R. Kelly, Beyoncé, Rihanna, August Alsina, just to name a few were no longer allowed to be played in my home nor my car. Does this seem a bit extreme? Yes, but this is what happens after you have been plagued with so many spirits of your own along with generational curses, God has to purge you of the old ratchet worldly way. This wasn't an easy process, but I had to begin to consume myself with the Father in Heaven. We were created to conform to whatever we consume daily. Plus, I would rather be spiritually minded.

Consuming myself with the Father, didn't stop the battle, but I began to see victory in my battles. In this place of purging, God also showed me many things about myself that needed to be cast out. I began to learn self-deliverance, and started laying hands on myself, binding spirits of rejection, jealousy, anger, lust, fear, even incubus. Some I could cast out with the help of the Holy Spirit, others had to be cast out by a deliverance minister, and incubus I had to battle for freedom in the dream world, by denying him, I even had a physical fight with him in my dream. He absolutely believed I was his property, but it was time to show him I am a daughter of the King and evict him.

Chapter Sixteen

Wow, I Have a Purpose!

If you didn't know, let me tell you, God still speaks. When God began speaking to me about my assignment, it came in parts. I had to put the pieces together. I am a dreamer and at times I have visions. At first my dreams were straight forward, but then after a while God began training me in dream interpretation. I knew I was called to deliverance because God revealed this to me in dreams as well. My first dream, was about my assignment in deliverance. This was after God led me to study deliverance and he began to train me in my dreams. In my first dream, there was a little girl who was demon possessed. I approached the little girl while she was in full manifestation, but my approach was wrong. I tried to show love and I reached my hands out as if to pick her up and I was saying, "Oh sweetheart what's wrong?" When I said that, the thing growled at me. I stepped back and the only thing I said was, "Y'all better get that thing!" It went from me being afraid to me approaching the spirit without fear, speaking with authority and casting the demon out. One dream I was walking down the street and God used me to cast demons out of a group of women. I knew I was called to women because in all the dreams I had regarding my assignment, I dealt with women of all ages.

During this season of dreams, is when God began to ask me, "Do You Trust Me?" At times we think we do, when truthfully, we have no idea what that means. There was an orphan spirit dwelling in me and God took me through a series of training to be able to step out on faith and trust him more, so that I could do the things he was about to request me to do. What I would do is listen to every sermon I could on trusting God, Sonship, and the orphan spirit, and meditate on every scripture pertaining to God's love, His protection, His provision, and His promises. I would listen to, "The Daddy Song" by Dennis Jernigan daily. I hadn't listen to the song for a few days, but the Holy Spirit woke me up singing to my heart, "I'll have no other, for I love only. I'll never forsake you or leave you alone. I love you, oh how I love you." This is when that spirit began to break. This song reminded me of how I listened to the stranger's voice of doubt, failure and fear of death.

Although Abba Father is loving, compassionate, caring, forgiving, gives good gifts and merciful there is also a disciplinary side to our heavenly Father. The rod of correction will drive away foolishness and impart wisdom. Without knowing the correction side, we would just be lawless, doing whatever we want and believing there are no consequences for our actions. Without knowing the love of the Father, we become legalistic. To know our Father, is to know both sides. God's correction is not condemning, it's convicting and it comes with instruction to rectify the problem. Expect lots of correction, but remember it is all done in love. I have even been corrected and rebuked regarding my thoughts. You ask how do we control our thoughts? Well when a negative thought comes, you fight with the word of God. You begin to cast down imaginations and every high thing that exalts itself against the knowledge of God and bringing into captivity every thought to the obedience of Christ. Our thoughts are in seed form, and if we allow it to stay and meditate on it, it will take root. Every sin begins with a thought.

Then God began to train me on trusting him for provision and this wasn't just monetary. God would constantly speak Matthew 6:25-33. So, I read it and meditate it and decree it! And every time I set my need at the altar he met every one of them, but whenever I was slack at trusting, God was slack at answering. When I noticed this, it became easier to trust him. And it is still getting easier. We must remember whatever God is telling us to do, He will make provision for. The assignments God gives us to do are always beyond reach, and we look within ourselves and do not see how this THING we have imagined will come to pass. Let me tell you something!! If it is in your own strength and ability, it is not a God idea. If it takes some stretching, and faith walking without knowing where your foot will land… That's God. If you could do it in your own strength you wouldn't need God, now would you?

God dropped *Women of Now Faith* into my spirit. Initially this was a private group on Facebook that was for women seeking prayer, accountability, whoever had a word could share and much more. I started the Facebook group in August 2015. I always had a desire as well to mentor teen mothers. But during the stretching God revealed so much more. I began to get prophetic words about Women of Now Faith being a business. Women of NOW Faith is now a mentorship program, that helps you get set free from spiritual strongholds, building accountability, finding your purpose and pushes you into your destiny. My niece Krystal, my daughter Tiffany and one of my very own mentors Vicky saw visions of my mentorship program. If God is speaking to you about a purpose, please listen and despise not the day of small beginnings.

Mentoring is an amazing opportunity to teach all that you know and to grow. Believe it or not, I learn a lot from my mentees as well. God is always stretching me and teaching me new things. That's another thing, we must remain teachable. You don't know it all!

I want you all to realize you are not just here existing. Everything has a purpose. You say what can God make of you? You don't feel like you could amount to anything? You think you are trash, well even a trash can has a purpose. God created you with purpose and it's up to you to seek him and you will find out exactly what it is. As I said so many times already, God will take whatever held you captive and build on that very thing that was meant to destroy you. Watch God use your life to impact if not thousands, then millions of people. Think about what drives you, what about people and what breaks your heart the most? This is your calling. Don't say you're not into people. Well, if you're in to God and God is in you, then you must be in to people…. Because God is into people

Chapter Seventeen

From Larvae to Butterfly

As I said before I was raised in the church, and I was baptized with water at 10 years old, but my true salvation didn't take place until 2014. What I began to learn in 2014 was so much more different from what I was taught as a child. Even speaking in tongues were a nuisance in my church. Didn't know what deliverance was and the way we were taught about the devil almost made it seem as if he was more powerful and had more authority or us than God. I repented of everything I had ever done, knowing and unknowingly and I asked God to show me myself and to make me whole. What is repentance? Repentance is not just saying. "I'm Sorry," but it means to turn away from. I was ready to stop doing all the worldly things and live more spiritual. Since you believed, have you received? We believe that God is the father and that Jesus exists, but what do we believe about the Holy Ghost/Spirit. Most people think the Holy Ghost is something you CATCH, while in service and you get this feeling of happy and you want to dance or take off running. I believe the Holy Spirit is a bit grieved by this. The Holy Spirit is a gift that you receive into your life. He comes to dwell IN YOU, to teach you, speak to you, lead you, guide you, and comfort you. When the Holy Spirit comes to dwell in you, you begin to change. Not that your life does full change in one day, but the change in you is evolutionary. The more you spend time with God and listen to the Holy Spirit's leading you begin to look more like Jesus.

Going forward from repentance to salvation then it is time to learn who we are. Learning who we are in Christ is the most important step for a believer. It teaches us mostly how important we are to God and how he is so invested in us. Fear is the greatest attack of the enemy on a believer, because he fears you coming into your identity. Our identity shows us that we have nothing to fear, not the future, not failure, not divination, not anything. It is important that we understand how God's perfect love cast out fear. This does not mean that we will never feel fear, but when we meet fear, we can remember who we belong to and how much God loves us, how much he is committed to us and his divine protection THEN we can cast out fear. If fear didn't exist we would not have to cast it out.

 I believe once we truly make a bold decision to truly follow Christ, He begins to give us personal promises. These promises can come through the Holy Spirit while you are in your secret place with God and you are open and ready to hear him. It may come in a dream or vision or through a prophetic vessel, just to name a few avenues. Now before I go further about the promises of God let me touch on prophets quickly. A lot of the time we condemn prophets, by calling them false because what they spoke to us didn't manifest. I believe we expect for the manifestation to fall out of the sky. We are to have faith in what is spoken to us, because Faith without works is dead. Has God already done all that he said he was going to do? Absolutely. It's our job to find out what is our assignments or preparation process for it to manifest. God is not our personal genie, and we can't expect him to make us prosperous or give us the desires of our heart, unless we are prepared and ready. Would you give your child a million bucks if he is already irresponsible? NO! You already know they would blow it. So why would God give us anything we are not ready for. Let us not get mad at the prophet because he spoke a word from the Lord that didn't manifest. The question is what are you doing to bring it to pass.

Back to the promises of God. The first time I ever heard God speak was in my secret place. I was awakened in the middle of the night and couldn't go back to sleep. I remember being taught that when you are up in the middle of the night, God wants to speak to you. I laid in the bed on my face and I said, "Lord, here I am. Speak to my heart." This was my first time taking the time out to hear God for myself. I believe he has always spoken to me, I just didn't know it. As soon as I laid on my face, I began to bubble up with words. These words were a promise for the future, and he also spoke it with a condition. Meaning, if you do this, then you will receive the promise. When God speaks into our lives, he is giving us something to focus on and look forward to. God will begin to take us through the process to receive all that He has for us. This process doesn't always feel good. During the process, you must become focused on the words God has spoken. It MUST become our motivation to press forward.

Begin to ask God to show you, yourself. I remember I did this and what I saw in myself was not pretty at all. It was pure ugliness, jealousy, bitterness, fear, rejection, unforgiveness etc. The great and awesome part about this, is that you see and you become hateful of it, then God begins to work these things out of you. For some, it may be a long process, maybe even a lifetime process other may dissipate speedily. But nonetheless you are aware and now God can handle these spirits.

What is our part in this? Cultivating a relationship with God. How do you do that? I'm glad you asked. By not just reading your bible, but studying your bible, along with daily prayer and devotion with God. When you sit down to study always have pen and paper because God will speak to you through scripture. You start off by asking God to give you revelation and understanding. I love to pray Ephesians 1:17-19 over myself before reading. Remember praying the word of God is always effective prayer. Allow God to take you on a journey and he will show you great things in the bible that you can apply to your life as well as help others. During prayer and devotion, find you a secluded area away from noise and distractions and you talk to God and sit quietly and allow him to speak back to you. You do not have to start off spending four hours in your prayer closet, but devote yourself to 10 minutes and allow God to do the increase. Trust me spending time with God is not boring.

Meditating scriptures and memorization is important as well. The more Word you have in you, the more God can speak to you. When I had to battle with anger I would find scriptures pertaining to anger. I would take the time out to memorize them, or have then on my wall, even on my computer at work and whenever I would feel the spirit of anger rising in me I would either pray these scriptures over myself or meditate on them. You can do this with any spiritual battle. If you are battling lust, fear, bitterness, hurt, rage, insecurity, breaking soul ties whatever it is you can find scripture to fight. In the beginning, it may seem like you are fighting these spirits every second, because they are trying to wear you out. But you must flip it and wear the evil spirits out. You will notice that the battle will decrease and you do not have to say those scriptures as often as you did when you first started. Stay in the race and Focus on God and the promises.

Forgiveness is a great part of your healing and deliverance process. I know what you are saying, but please remember you have a great work to do in the kingdom and God needs your heart pure. What we must understand that, we wrestle not against flesh and blood, but against principalities, against powers, against rules of the darkness of this world and spiritual wickedness in high places. So, it is not the people who are our enemies but the spirits that are operating through them. We must remember they need to be set free just as we do. We have all hurt someone in some way, but wouldn't you want to be forgiven? I had to practice praying for people who have hurt me. This prayer did not consist of "Lord, show them the errors of their ways or Lord you see what they did to me (Your Child) make 'em pay Lord!" But I prayed blessings over all family members that have hurt me, friends, people I have been in close relationship with and the like. This was a hard task at first, and my prayers didn't sound right. They were full of bitterness unforgiveness and hurt, but after practicing this daily, I felt a lift and my prayers over them changed dramatically and I could see them as God sees them. The enemy doesn't just use anybody to get you off your path. He will use people close to you that may have a great influence on you and they don't even know it, so you MUST love the person. We only have an enemy, but he is not human. They are satan and his imps. I pray God opens doors that no man can close in their lives. Open the windows of heaven, I pray a hedge of protection around them and their families. Just begin to pray and watch God do the rest.

Luke 6:28 say, bless those who curse you. Pray for those who mistreat you.

You will see that Bitterness is destroyed, hurt is removed, and you will be able to even sit in the same room with the person. Forgiveness is a release, as you release those feelings, you release people. NOW! What forgiveness is not! It's not ignorance, nor stupidity. Many people believe if you forgive someone we have to accept them back fully into our lives. This is not always true, you can forgive people and move on.

When God purges you, you may find yourself being removed from family, friends, jobs, churches, neighborhoods and many more. God begins to remove everything out of your life that is not like him. It could feel as if you're alone at first, but just hold on. God is taking you higher, have no fear and embrace the process. I discussed earlier in the book that I had to guard my gates. This part of the purging helps to clean and purify you so that you hear God more clearly. You began to think more like him. My children and I were mocked for this. My cousin Cynthia admitted that she felt I was taking it to far, but she began to understand later, and now God has called her on a purge of her own. My children loved horror films and sci-fi movies but I stopped allowing them to watch these types of movies. My children don't have nightmares anymore and they get more prophetic dreams about their future. My 6-year-old had a dream and told me God told her, he was removing fear from her.

God also began to bring people into life. Those that walk in the fear and admiration from the Lord, they have had to rebuke, correct, exhort and pray for me. They are Detris, Katrena, Faith, Rockie, Doranda, Cynthia and Quadetra. God replaced the friends I had with Godly women that pushed me and continue to push me into purpose and assignment, upon assignment.

What I learned in my journey of life? Being a child of God we don't get away with nothing. Lol... I would be at work and I would get called into the office about the same things others in my clinic were doing. My cell phone on my desk, going to get breakfast, almost seemed like whenever I would breath I was called in the office. Now years ago, when this would happen, I would go toe to toe with the supervisors and co-workers, even threaten to write grievances. Not understanding I was in training, also being my own God and trying to fight my own battles. Once I learned to remove myself and allow God to step in I saw the power of God fighting my battles. I also learned, being a child of God I can't do everything that everybody else does. I have a different standard to uphold, so being called in the office stopped bothering me and I began to understand that it was only making me a better more efficient employee.

Part of getting away with nothing means "No Secrets." In Chapter Eleven I wrote about My Daughter Dacia's alleged father, taking a DNA test behind my back. This was my biggest kept secret, and the Holy Spirit had been pressing in on me for the past few years to tell my daughter the truth. The only person that I gave this information to was my oldest daughter. For the past 2 years, I had been hinting around with Dacia that Calvin may not being her father. I didn't know how to come out and say it, until Dacia grew a desire to move with her dad to California, but when it came time, he would make excuses like, "Well, we may be moving back to Chicago." I noticed her hurt and about a year ago I exposed the truth that Calvin was not her father, but we went on about life normally. I had not yet told Calvin that I told Dacia the truth. But in October 2016, we were at World Changers Conference for my church All Nations Worship Assembly and Apostle began to call out demonic spirits that people were plagued with and one of the Evangelist walked over to Dacia and began to prophecy to her regarding suicidal thought and the fact she feels abandoned by her father.

The very next day I texted Calvin to explain what was going on with our daughter. He didn't answer immediately, but eventually called back. Calvin said, "There is an issue that needs to be addressed that we seemed to have swept under the rug." I was prepared and I already knew what this was about. I said, "Are you speaking of that DNA test, I have already begun to tell her the truth because I notice suddenly you began to change." He then said he wanted to do another DNA test through the courts, because he felt that the first DNA was an at home test and they were new and didn't know if they were accurate. I told him, I am game for that, but again Calvin was trying to do this without her understanding what was happening. First of all, she is 15 years old, how in the world do you take a 15-year old somewhere and she not ask questions about what is going on. I refused and told him NO, I will not continue to hide this from Dacia if we go, she will know exactly what is going on. Calvin asked he had I talk to Fred regarding being the possible father, I informed him, that I did tell Fred, and Fred said to let him know what he needs to do, but Calvin chose to remain Dacia's dad and I never contacted Fred about it after that. Calvin said he was making a trip to Chicago on business and he would get together with Dacia and me so we could go and begin the process.

I then called Fred and told him what the deal was and he remembered our conversation years ago regarding Dacia possibly being his daughter. Fred told me, "Let Calvin get the DNA, let me know the results, but I don't need a DNA, I am going to continue to do exactly what I been doing." What Fred meant when he said this? He has always filled that father spot for Dacia, and Keke. What he does for his biological daughter Tiffany, he does for them. Fred has never made a difference in them. He never said I am coming to get Tiffany, but he always called and said, "Nikki I want to get my babies for the weekend or the summer."

Calvin was flying in to Chicago two weeks later and he said, he would come and talk to Dacia and set up for us to go somewhere to get the DNA test. The day before Calvin was to come to Chicago I called him, but got no answer. I then sent a text to ask if we were still on for the weekend and I still got no response. The next day I called and got no answer AGAIN! I noticed Dacia would text Calvin and get no answer as well. My child was hurting, she felt abandoned and rejected. One morning I was on my way to work and Tiffany called me and let me know Dacia said she hates her life and don't be sad if she doesn't return then stormed out of the house. It took us a while to find her, but when my neighbor found her. I told her either she was going to open up, or we are going into the hospital. She told me, she saw Calvin would go to his sons' basketball games and that he brought the older sibling Jay Jay a car and Christmas past and she got nothing from him and she calls him and he doesn't respond often. Then, I had no other choice but to tell her about the plan he had to come and talk to her, but he just simply ran away from confronting this issue.

I am thankful for the community that Dacia has to get through this tough time. She has her mentor Rockie, Fred and family that love her so much and are always here for her. We know that this is a process, but we are moving ahead swiftly. I used this story as an example because secrets are ammunition for the devil. He holds them over your head to condemn you and it makes it extremely hard to move forward. Whatever is in the dark, please bring it to the light. Fear not, there is no problem too big for our God to fix.

God will give you a new name, a new nature. You become a new creature in Christ. Now, you will have people come to you and try to bring up the old you but all you have to do is smile and say, "That person is dead, the new me has been resurrected." I LOVE the metamorphosis of the butterfly. How something so ugly transforms into something so beautiful. I can compare my life to this because the process that we go through when God changes us is like this. During the process you feel hidden, and in this hidden place (the cocoon) is where the change happens. Once you come out of that hidden place (the cocoon) you come out beautiful ready for all that God has prepared for you!

154

About the Author

   LaShaneika "Nikki" Franklin, an author and public speaker, is the founder of the *Women of Now Faith* mentorship program with the mission of bringing women, teen mothers, young adults, and youth into their identity in Christ Jesus. She provides accountability partnership, deliverance ministry and the maintenance of spiritual freedom. Just as God "snatched" her out of the hands of satan, she is dedicated to being a noble vessel in the assignment of snatching others out of darkness. Visit www.womenofnowfaith.com for more information.

Interested in publishing your own book?
Visit
livingwordpublishers.com

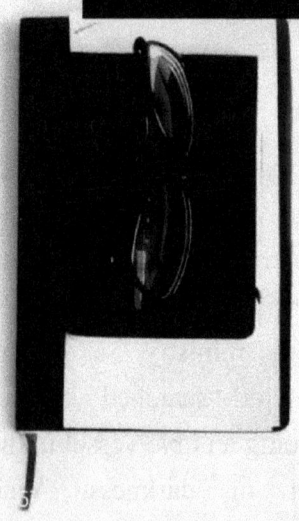

www.ingramcontent.com/pod-product-compliance
Lightning Source LLC
Chambersburg PA
CBHW071743150426
43191CB00010B/1670